Boomer  Babes

St. Martin's Griffin

New York

Boomer Babes

A
Woman's
Guide
to the
New
Middle
Ages

Linda Stasi *and*

Rosemary Rogers

BₐₜT 2\11\98 9/295

305.244
STA

Design by Songhee Kim

Library of Congress Cataloging-in-Publication Data

Stasi, Linda
    Boomer babes : a woman's guide to the new middle
    ages / by Linda Stasi and Rosemary Rogers.—1st ed.
        p.   cm.
    ISBN 0-312-18061-6
    1. Middle aged women—United States.   2. Baby boom
generation—United States.   3. Middle age—Humor.
I. Rogers, Rosemary.   II. Title
HQ1059.5.U5S73   1998
305.244—dc21   97-38274
                                                              CIP

First St. Martin's Griffin Edition: March 1998
10   9   8   7   6   5   4   3   2   1

296'
1103

To my mother, Florence Stasi, who made me possible

and Jess, who made me probable

and Sid—totally impossible

L. S.

For a great mother (Rose Rogers),

a great daughter (Nell Rogers Michlin),

a great sister (Kathy Rogers McKeever),

and a great guy (Bob Downey)

R. R.

contents

Old age may be no place for sissies,
but middle age is *definitely* no place for
baby boomers.

Boomer Babes at Fifty: Still Ready to Rock

*I am not twentyish, I am not thirtyish. Three months
ago I was forty years old. Forty. Four oh—That
slipped. I hadn't quite made up my mind to admit it.
Now I feel as though I've suddenly taken all my
clothes off.*
—Margo Channing, ALL ABOUT EVE

Admitting to forty in the fifties was as bad as admitting to
er, ah, um, fifty at the millennium.

Will we women of the sex, drugs, and rock and roll generation face fifty without flipping out? You're kidding, right?
Are there no plastic surgeons? Are there no mud wraps?

Not that we're going to take it lying down, mind you.
Hey—we jettisoned girdles and bobby pins as a way of life,
so we certainly aren't going to go gentle into the land of Depends. We ain't our mothers, we ain't our older sisters, and
we ain't going down without a fight.

Don't forget that we fought in the streets in the sixties with rock music as our soundtrack. Who said war had to be hell?

The first wave of female baby boomers, those of us born between 1946 and 1955—nineteen million strong—ditched the notion of becoming Mrs. Jim Anderson. We figured Father *didn't* know best.

Hell no, we didn't want to go *anywhere* in a hairdo, a panty girdle, and a shirtwaist dress.

Okay. Now millions of us are looking fifty in the face (literally and figuratively). We're finding that getting older isn't the problem, it's *looking* older that pisses us off. Let's face it, looking older was always the first step on the disposable dame ladder. You know—disposed of by husbands, lovers, employers, children, and worst of all, even cosmetics companies! You can live without a man, but you can't live without mascara.

Screw that.

For all of us nineteen million women who tuned in, turned on, and dropped out, it's time to redefine, redesign, and reinvent ourselves. Again. After all, we did it the first time around with no role models—the only famous women we knew were movie stars, the wives of movie stars, and the wives of powerful husbands.

And even then, only the movie stars seemed to be having any sex . . . until, of course, they lost their looks and killed themselves.

If a woman did something to change the world back then,

she inevitably ended up looking like Eleanor Roosevelt. If a woman looked like a babe, no one would have taken her seriously.

So here we are—too old to be young and way too young to be old. We'd tell you to steal this book, but we need the money. We're not getting any younger (or is that older?). Instead, buy this manifesto for the new middle ages, a guidebook to staying hip and hot without flipping out.

After all, we're still ready to rock!

two

Fifty Good Reasons

to Turn Fifty

1. It's better than dying.
2. If you make a mistake, it doesn't shatter your confidence in your own judgment. Instead you now say, "I made a mistake. Big deal. I didn't kill anyone." (Leave the last part out if you actually did kill someone.)
3. You don't get embarrassed easily anymore. Blunders that in your youth would have prompted you to enter a witness protection program now roll off your psyche. (The only exception to this is if you simultaneously rip your dress and fall while accepting an Academy Award.)

4. Liberating phrases are now part of your vocabulary: "It's not my problem." "Who cares?" "Get over yourself." "So sue me." "What an asshole." "F#$@ it!"

5. You picked a good time to turn fifty. Millions of other women are doing it these days, and the face of fifty has definitely changed and changed radically. Think about this: In 1950, in *Sunset Boulevard*, Norma Desmond was fifty. In 1998, in real life, Susan Sarandon is fifty-two.

6. You now realize that you don't have to send Christmas cards or make your bed unless you actually *want* to.

7. You've stopped trying to change people.

8. You have your own voice. Now when you think and speak, the opinions are really your own and not those of some boyfriend, girlfriend, or a grown-up who knows more than you.

9. You judge yourself by your own standards. For example, "Am I the fattest person who ever lived?"

10. You don't doubt yourself or who you are and rarely, if ever, have an *Asshole Attack*. (Translation: when you wake up the next morning wishing you could take back the night before.)

11. Now when you feel competitive with other women, it's about important issues, namely, who earns a bigger salary and who has better stock options.

12. More than ever before, you enjoy the company of other women, especially other women around your age. After all, who besides you (who's over three feet tall anyway) wets her pants?

13. Fifty means never having to say you're sorry (except when you've run someone over).

14. You don't care if your in-laws like you, hate you, or even know you exist.

15. You no longer care if your mother approves of your boyfriend. Or your husband. Or your best friend.

16. You're finally careful about your diet. You have to be. Remember: "What doesn't kill you will make you stout."

17. You've finally achieved true sexual liberation. You have to do only what you want, when you want, and with whom you want.

18. You realize that the only people with true power over you work for the IRS.

19. Your short-term memory is so shot that you forget if you lied about your age to the person you're talking to. This is okay because your memory is such a memory that you soon forget you're embarrassed.

20. They now have fat-free Carvel.

21. The $6 manicure. Anywhere. Anytime. Anyplace.

22. You no longer care if people think you're a: lesbian, bisexual, trisexual, asexual. Or that you: came from the wrong side of the tracks or tracts, went to Ed & Larry University, didn't go to college at all, haven't read Sartre (in French), don't like to cook/do like to cook, and everything else that used to make you feel like shit.

23. Instead of furtive peeks at *The Enquirer* at the supermarket checkout, you can now read it shamelessly on public transportation.

24. You have finally realized that Audrey Hepburn was a walking eating disorder with fashion know-how.

25. Nobody—unless he is brandishing a machete—is especially intimidating anymore.

26. You no longer feel the need to sleep with someone you don't even want to have lunch with.

27. A facial still works.

28. You can enjoy vegetarian food without worrying about falling into the hands of the Communists.

29. You can go to a spa without feeling like you're trapped inside *The Women.*

30. Being alone means that you enjoy your own company, not that you're a lonely woman alone with her cats.

31. "The only thing we have to fear is fear itself." Okay, so we didn't make that one up. But you can now laugh at things that used to scare the pants off you: broken bra straps, Kenny Keegan, algebra, boys seeing your underpants, sororities, psoriasis, the A-bomb, stains—particularly under your arms and on the back of your skirt—and being dateless on Saturday night, prom night, or New Year's Eve. Then there was the escaped murderer who left his hook of a hand on your car door, and you found cockroaches in your beehive hairdo.

32. Baseball caps instead of hairdos.

33. Clogs are back.

34. You're proud of your ordering-out skills.

35. You have no desire to have blue water in your toilet bowl.

36. You don't need to keep up with all the new dances.

37. You're in better shape now than when you were at twenty-five. Or at least you should be.

38. You've stopped smoking. Or at least you should have.

39. When you say, "Don't let the door hit you in the ass on your way out," you're talking to your husband.

40. You now feel free to openly despise people who use the words "gal" and "fella."

41. You don't have to call home on business trips.

42. You no longer care when your ex threatens to sue you for custody. Let him—the tuition is killing you.

43. Platform shoes are back.

44. Leggings, the forgiving fashion are here.

45. You've dated so much that it takes you only fifteen minutes to know what's what and what gives and who doesn't.

46. You can buy your own jewelry.

47. You can take yourself on vacation.

48. You can buy your own car—the one *you* want this time.

49. You can buy your own house and live in it with anyone or no one.

50. Been there, done that, and can do it again. But only if you want to.

three

Ten Commandments for Preserving Babedom

I. DON'T LIE ABOUT YOUR AGE

There are many reasons to come clean here. For one thing, unless you scored 800 on your math SATs, the math will kill you. And do you really want to go through making all that fake ID again? It would be beyond humiliating to get caught lying about your age, plus it would create suspicion that you might be older than you actually are. So unless you have the balls of the Gabors, we recommend that you obey this commandment.

Why not take a deep breath, stand up straight, look them straight in the eye, and come out with the truth?

Remember, there are a lot of us. Think back to your horribly overcrowded third-grade classroom—seventy kids huddled under their desks to escape atomic devastation. Every kid in that classroom, including the boy who used to sneak a peek at your underpants during air raid drills and the girl with the Toni who was never tardy, will be turning the big 5-0.

2. DON'T LOSE TOO MUCH WEIGHT

To paraphrase Catherine Deneuve: When a woman is over forty, she has to choose between her ass and her face. The face should win. Losing too much weight will make you look not only older but scarier. Despite what we've been told our whole lives, you *can* be too thin. Remember, the woman who made this up—the Duchess of Windsor—was married to the man who would be queen.

Also, the thinner you are, the greater risk you run of getting osteoporosis and spending your twilight years shaped like a question mark.

Besides, who would you rather look like—Deneuve or the Duchess?

3. DON'T GAIN TOO MUCH WEIGHT

If you were all excited by Commandment 2, calm down. We just said don't get skinny—we didn't say you should classify Dunkin' Donuts as a food group.

Meat on your bones is good; fat on your meat is not.

4. SPEND MORE MONEY ON UNDERWEAR AND SHOES

Both keep you up and keep you from looking bent over. With any luck, you'll reap double lotto: floozie pumps with the souls of sneakers; industrial-strength undies with the heart of a Paris bordello.

5. UPDATE YOUR IMAGE

It's not how you feel, it's how you look. If you don't want to look about fifty years older than you already are, please remember that in the war on aging, less is more! In other words, the more you age, the less gunk you should pile on. (See Chapter 18, "Making Up to Make It Big: The Babe's Complete Guide to Makeup.") First, don't lay on the foundation with a trowel—it highlights the lines. Second, ditch the frosted and colored eye shadow. Third, unless you're the wife of a fallen Evangelist minister, avoid pink blush and brown lip liner. Fourth, for the sake of everything that's holy, remember that under-eye concealer is supposed to conceal circles, not give you big white rings. Try finding a shade that actually comes close to human flesh.

Finally, if your hairdo closely resembles that of Miss Texas, you have automatically added ten years to your age. (See Chapter 17, "Hair Raising: The Babe's Complete Guide to Hair.")

6. IN THE NAME OF GOD, DRESS SIMPLY

The following garments should be avoided like a large plague of locusts:

- Blackglama—you're too young
- Crop tops—you're too old
- Culottes. Period.
- Tops with animals printed on them
- Cowboy hats
- Ruffles—anywhere, anytime, anyplace, on anything
- Turquoise (the color, not jewelry)
- Coral (the color and especially the jewelry)
- Two-piece jogging suit
- Blue stretch pants
- Shawls, capes, and big lady-editor scarves
- Shirts that are too long, short, pleated, full, tight, or coral
- Big necklaces, unless they're big with diamonds

7. MOISTURIZE EVERYTHING ALL THE TIME

And that includes from the inside out. So drink eight glasses—at least—of water a day. Get a humidifier, and keep it clean and keep it on.

8. HALF-GLASSES ARE FOR HALF-ASSES

If you need reading glasses—and we know you do—please somehow control yourself and do not under any circumstances succumb to buying—or, worse, wearing—half-glasses. It's like wearing a sandwich board for the AARP. You may possibly never have sex again if you ignore this warning.

A subcategory to avoid like a touch of Ebola is big glasses with the dipping side pieces. The only person who can get away with wearing these is Sophia Loren—the greatest babe who ever lived—and the only reason she even wears them is because she owns the company, or part of it, or something.

9. GET MORE SLEEP AT NIGHT AND MEDITATE IN THE MORNING

Let's face it, you simply can't do the things to blissful excess that you used to do (with the possible exception of sex) and still look good.

You'll sleep better at night if you start the day meditating for at least fifteen minutes. It will give you time to yourself and with yourself. Need inspiration to get started? Put on an old Beatles song. Better yet, *Valley of the Sun* meditation/ motivation tapes by Dick Sutphin are fabulous.

10. TAKE A WALK, LADY

If you don't force yourself to walk at least twenty minutes a day, you will be old before your time. Babes are in shape— or else they wouldn't be called babes (in fact, they wouldn't be called at all).

Here's why else you need to walk it off:

Walking twenty minutes a day will make you ten pounds thinner a year from now.

Walking is better than running, because running makes everything that's starting to fall, fall faster.

It's free.

Ten Commandments for Preventing Old Fartdom

I. KEEP LISTENING TO ROCK

Rock is our music. We came of age with it, and we should come of middle age with it.

Proviso: Even if you hate Rage Against the Machine, saying it out loud can immediately make you sound like Ed Sullivan introducing the Beatles (or, as he put it, the Beet-uls).

But more important, always remember that it is better to bite off your own leg than to listen to any orchestrated version of any Led Zeppelin song.

Corollary: If you must listen to corny rock and roll, please do so in the privacy of your own home. This includes doo-wop, the Mamas and the Papas, and especially Michael Bolton.

2. NEVER WEAR MORE THAN ONE DROP OF PERFUME

And never wear even one drop of Giorgio.

3. AVOID OLD-LADY EXPRESSIONS

The following phrases should never come out of your mouth:

- "Unhook my brassiere."
- "My ankles are swollen."
- "Sock it to me, baby."
- "I have a coupon for it."
- "That looks sharp."
- "That's a man's job."
- "Coordinating wardrobe"
- "Mediterranean bedroom set"
- "*Peau de soie* shoes"
- "He's dead, right?"
- "Iron curtain," "iron lung," "iron-poor blood"
- "Slacks"
- "The kids got sick on me."
- "Rouge"

- "She must have had some work done" (generally said while watching *The Tonight Show*).
- "So, I put on some weight—what do you expect? I'm middle-aged, for Crissakes!"
- "My back is out."
- "Decoration day"
- "Beauty parlor," "pizza parlor," "funeral parlor," "ice cream parlor," anything, in fact, ending in "parlor," with the exception of "tatoo"
- "My podiatrist said . . ."

4. GET A COMPUTER

Like rock and roll, computers are here to stay. Buy one, use it, and get on-line. Being a computer illiterate keeps you frozen in time and out in the cold. As soon as you say, "I can't keep up with all this technology . . . I'm a dinosaur," you immediately look and sound like Mrs. Lawrence Welk. Don't think that it's gotten so far ahead of you that you'll never catch up. You will.

5. HIT THE ROAD, GIRLFRIEND

Take a road trip, drive too fast in bare feet, listen to music too loud, don't make reservations, sign in at motels under an assumed name (try a movie character), stop at diners, drink huge amounts of real coffee and real Coke, eat hot dogs and fries, and don't call your office.

6. AVOID THE FOLLOWING MEDIA LIKE CRAZY

- *Reader's Digest*
- *TV Guide* (It's bad enough to buy it, but if you find yourself highlighting it with a yellow marker, throw your television out. Now.)
- *The Christian Science Monitor*
- The 700 Club
- Infomercials (especially the ones with the man in the terrible sweaters)
- Lite FM
- Barbra Streisand CDs and movies
- Liza Minnelli concerts
- Any book with Fabio on the cover
- *Who's the Boss?* reruns
- *The Price Is Right*
- *Woodstock*, the movie—again
- *The Celestine Prophecy*
- Any movie score by Marvin Hamlisch

7. DON'T OPEN BUTTONS OR UNZIP ZIPPERS AFTER A GOOD MEAL

Kill yourself before ever uttering a postprandial "uffffffff," talking heartburn, let alone, God forbid, even mentioning gas.

8. KNOW WHEN TO HOLD 'EM, KNOW WHEN TO HIDE 'EM

DISCREETLY LEAVE LYING AROUND
THESE THINGS YOU USED TO HIDE

- Your diaphragm case
- Midol
- Tampons
- Birth control pills
- Sexy underwear

BOLDLY DISPLAY

- Magazines: *Details, Wired, Spin, Muscle & Fitness*
- CDs: Pantera, Cypress Hill, Pearl Jam, Helmet
- Shoes: Doc Martens
- Videos: *Pulp Fiction*
- Books: *The Rachel Papers*
- Eats: Rice Krispie treats
- Drinks: Samuel Adams beer
- Smokes: Cuban cigars

HIDE!!!!!!!!!

- AARP literature
- Metamucil
- Loving Care
- Nose-hair clippers
- Gas-X

- Your collection of 45s
- Correctol
- Wedding album
- Replens, K-Y jelly
- High school yearbook
- Pitted prunes
- Cast album of *Hair*
- Estrogen tablets

9. KNOW YOUR POSITION IN POLITE SOCIETY

When you lie on your side, does your stomach do the same? Let's be honest here. Once past forty, things that were formerly attached to your body seem to take on a life of their own. So special caution is needed when you assume the top position during sex—it's not just your jowls you need to worry about at this point.

There are, for example, the arms. Please, please don't do any excessive waving in short or, God forbid, sleeveless tops, if you suffer from the tragic malady known as Hadassah arms.

Stand in front of a full-length mirror wearing only your bra. Raise your right arm over your head. Wave wildly. If flapping noises occur, immediately start shopping for long-sleeved bathing suits.

Then there's posture: Have you ever caught yourself sitting with your legs even slightly apart, when crossed-at-the-knees was always natural. Or worse—assuming a stance that involves sloping your shoulders while simultaneously thrusting your abdomen forward, like a big dumb *S*. There's only one solution: Ask your best friend, or even a total stranger, to kill you.

10. AVOID THE COMPANY OF OLD FARTS

There's nothing that will make you older faster than hanging out with people who embrace old fartdom like an old friend.

They've been waiting their whole lives to give up. In their youth, they were burdened by the stuff of youth—the challenges, the need to experience, to travel, to taste the good, the bad, the ugly of life. Chronological age has nothing to do with it. They are the Barney Fifes of life—born old.

Avoid them like a bad smell.

Men, Part 1:

What Was I *Thinking* of?

These are the chapters we've all been waiting for—the man chapters.

And believe it or not, the news is good. Yes, Virginia, there *is* love after forty and fifty. And sex. And laughs. And we're finally old enough to enjoy all three at the same time. This might be because we're finally mature enough to appreciate being appreciated. There had to be *something* good about getting older and no longer having boobs of steel.

If, however, you are one of the three reported women in America who are still happily married to hubby number one, please move on to the menopause chapter. This chapter is strictly for boomer babes who still haven't nailed the right guy, or may have but don't know it. Hey—even though we should have figured out by now that we don't necessarily need someone to be happy, we can still be happy with someone.

THE WAY WE WERE AND THE WAY IT WASN'T

It used to be much easier. We *knew* what the perfect man should be: tall, rich, handsome, sexy, brave, and hugely successful. In other words, your basic Marlboro man with a couple of bucks and a convertible. All the things we figured girls couldn't be.

Of course, nobody ever told us that 99 percent of guys couldn't be that either. And nobody told *them*. It was a tough gig all around—until the Vic Berman Syndrome swept across America in 1967 faster than a fire in a falsie factory.

For those uninitiated in the Vic Berman Syndrome (otherwise known as VBS—not to be confused with PMS, HIV, HRT, or PBS), a brief description might be in order. VBS was a phenomenon, born of the hippie movement, by which even the nerdiest of guys—who otherwise would have remained virgins until their mothers died—could have sex *anytime, anywhere,* and with *anyone.* This unbearable good luck could belong to any guy. All he had to do was let the hair on his head and face grow and spout some sort of anti-war ideology while wearing army fatigues.

For reasons we hope never fully to understand—including
the pill and liberation—it was suddenly uncool to refuse
anyone who was cool. Liberation?! This was about as liberating as a panty girdle.

What all of this amounted to is one truism for which we
are all responsible: The sixties basically ruined sex. We
seemed to have gone temporarily insane. Girls slept with
guys they wouldn't go out on a date with.

Maybe that's why drugs became so popular—just so nobody, and we mean *nobody*, would have to remember that
she'd actually slept with Vic Berman.

Tragically, many of us actually married Vic Berman and
his ilk, only to wake up one morning to find—yes!—a nerd
in the bed. Thus was born the first collective women's wail
heard from Bangor to Burbank: "What was I *thinking* of?"

Reluctant to admit this monumental blunder out loud,
we often stayed married and even gave birth to small
Berman-like critters. We loved them and nurtured them re-
gardless, and prayed to God that they would not one day ask
for a ham radio kit or a pocket protector. Fortunately, the
Berman genes often turned out to be as recessive as the
Berman hairline.

We could go on and on—the men we married and the
men we didn't and the men we should have married. Okay,
then, we will.

We were the first wives of Vic and Marlboro, plus an as-
sortment of cheapskates, deadbeats, and nice guys who outgrew us and nice guys whom we outgrew. We married men

who belonged in camps for the oversexed and men who needed to be pried loose from the TV to get started.

There were men who wanted children, and men who didn't, and men who didn't know what they wanted. Come to think of it, neither did we. What were we *all* thinking of? We certainly couldn't blame it on the fact that we never had sex before.

We wanted to marry Jim Morrison. They wanted to marry Michelle Phillips. Of course, Jim Morrison ended up as just another tub in a tub, and Michelle Phillips had relationships with so many junkies she could have opened her own yard.

But all we knew then was that we wanted to live the hip version of *Father Knows Best*. The oxymoron as lifestyle.

If the sixties was improbable, it was more probable than what we set ourselves up for later in . . . the lost years—the seventies!

We are personally horrified to discover that there are whole years missing in the old memory bank. Quick. What were you doing in 1977?

What can you *really* say about a decade that featured cheese fondue? This was the decade, remember, in which Paul McCartney stopped being a Beatle and became, instead, a wimp in Wings. This was the decade that spawned disco and the horrible clothes that looked good only on John Travolta. All three, by the way, are back.

Most significantly, this was the decade in which, for reasons too awful to contemplate, we all slept with men who wore leisure suits and had terrifying perms. Don't lie—you did it, and you know you did it.

And those men! By 1972, men who mysteriously looked like Robert Evans began populating the earth. Some may say it was an invasion from the planet ManTan, others deny these allegations. What we know for sure is that even normal men became so sleazy that when we went out with them we felt prompted to put paper down on the car seat.

Then there was the spiritual sleaze of instant analysis. Vic Berman met Werner Erhardt, and it wasn't a pretty story. What can you *ever* say about a decade in which a Jewish encyclopedia salesman took on a Nazi name and formed a new religion? What in God's *name* could we have been thinking of?

But we were nonetheless convinced that this time we were *really* liberated. Unfortunately, somehow we were still sleeping with Vic Berman! Same guy, different suit. Same rhetoric, different topic. Same results.

Some of us, blessedly, were in marriages. Not necessarily blissful marriages, but marriages that probably saved us from the scourge of the eighties—the dreaded herpes.

In the eighties, one out of two American marriages failed, and sexually transmitted diseases (STDs) made it to the cover of *Time*. Deals replaced sex. This was the decade of dollar decadence and Gordon Gecko—the Wall Street ideal.

Billions and billions were made, mostly by three people who worked day and night to undermine the entire economic structure of the United States for their own personal gain. Moguls became the new male sex symbols.

Michael Milken (aka Vic Berman) must right now have a basement that looks like Scrooge McDuck's—because all that money that everybody made seems to be gone. He must have it because we sure don't. Do you?

And those drugs. Was there anything more boring than cokespeak? Those late-night conversations that were in many respects exactly like the parallel play your kids were having on the playground during the day. Nobody cared what anybody was saying, and nobody shut up.

Yuppies ruled the earth with their hard bodies, and seventy-hour work weeks. They ruined life as we knew it. Sure they could work seventy hours. They were fueled by coke and mesquite-grilled free-range chicken.

It was chic for guys to become commitmentphobes. Suddenly, they didn't want to sleep with us! The term "emotionally unavailable" became a whole lifestyle. Incredibly, Vic Berman needed his space. The odd thing is that after he said this, he couldn't wait to fill up his space with a twenty-year-old cellulite-free Swede.

So what did we learn from all this?

GOLDEN RULE #1

Never marry a man before he's had at least one midlife crisis. Never get married again unless you've had at least one of your own.

Men, Part 2:
Mr. Wrong's in the Right Suit

> **GOLDEN RULE #2**
> The right man in the wrong suit beats the wrong man
> in the right suit.

Hard as it may be to put away your prejudice and not faint at the sight of a man in yellow pants, you must. For the moment, anyway. The truth is, the majority of really great ones have never figured out how to pull themselves together. They resist change and can't figure out why someone would pay $60 to get his hair trimmed when he can pay $10. It's okay, really. Besides, at this stage, who needs the competition?

If you ignore Golden Rule #2, tragically, you will be doomed to recurring bouts of VBS. Here, then, is a checklist of the good, the bad, and the impossible. First, the guys who look so right on paper and are so wrong in real life.

RIGHT SUIT/WRONG MAN #1: THE SERIAL MONOGAMER

S/M for short—literally. He is the guy who hasn't been unmarried or uncommitted since the ninth grade. He's committed, all right. It's just that he's always committed to a different woman. If he's not making himself miserable, he's making you miserable.

He always thinks it's better on the other side of the street, so he crosses and walks the same way on the other side, until he thinks it's better on the other side of the street and crosses it again. Thing is, he's always walking the same straight line, never stepping on the cracks.

To say he's compulsive is an understatement. He makes compulsive look sloppy. He always does the same thing— even in his relationships, especially in his relationships. Take his wife-swapping habit (wherein he swaps last year's version for a new, undented model). Even then, he just *thinks* he's changing the woman when he finds a new one, when in fact he's changing only the face.

Once ensconced, he immediately begins doing the same

exact things with the new one that he did with the old one.

He goes to the same places, picks on her for the same exact things he picked on his ex for, wears the same style of clothing, and orders the same food in restaurants. He's been telling the same jokes and stories since birth, which may be why he constantly seeks new long-term relationships. He doesn't mean to cause harm, but he's run out of stories!

He generally finds a new woman before leaving the old one. Perhaps he can't stand the fact that she refuses to alphabetize the spices.

The scenario: You meet him, and he sure looks good. He is neither a nerd nor a god. He's a generic good-looking guy. He's charming in his own way. He looks a little vulnerable. He hints that he's been hurt in the past. (He's been hurt all right—by dividing up the property.)

If he's not married, he's probably living with someone. If he *is* married, he'll admit it right up-front. He also admits that he's in the process of "getting divorced." This thought never actually occurred to him until he met you five minutes ago—but what the hell, he means it now. After all, you are different from every other woman who's ever been different before.

It's tough not to get swept up in his frenzy. He *will* leave his wife or girlfriend for you. But then *you're* stuck with him—until he finds someone new he can't live without.

Even so, his leaving leaves you bereft. Besides loving the guy, you actually liked him, too. Now you're saying to yourself, "Why did I think that if he did it to her, he wouldn't do it to me, too?" Because you didn't, that's why. You didn't fall in love with him because he seemed like such a huge loser, for God's sake. You fell in love with him because he seemed like the first really committed man you'd met in a very long time.

Scratch it up and move on.

CHARACTERISTICS OF THE BREED

Neat: Combs his hair a lot.

Habitual: His women generally have the same job, or are at least in the same profession, and they look somewhat the same. He's one of the few men of the baby boom generation who drink martinis. He did then and he does now—and he makes the same "witty" martini jokes he heard his father say when he was growing up. If you hear a man say, "Just wave the Vermouth over the glass," run for the hills.

GOLDEN RULE #3

If he's not married by his fortieth birthday, he'll marry you only if he suddenly discovers a prostate problem.

WRONG MAN/RIGHT SUIT #2: THE TIN MAN: EVERYTHING BUT A HEART

He is the anti-Christ of commitment. When he was a little boy, he was the kid who squirmed when hugged and kissed and really didn't seem to need anyone very much. As an adult, he may have the obligatory first marriage under his belt but is really and truly the professional bachelor who actually *resents* being loved. A shrink would call him a primary narcissist, but we call him the Tin Man, or just a big pain in the ass.

The Tin Man spent his adolescence hunkered over *Playboy* in the bathroom, eyeing busty blondes and thinking, "That's for me!" He watched ratpack movies and visualized himself in a small fedora at a jaunty angle saying ring-a-ding-ding every time one of those busty blondes walked by, which of course was all the time.

A swinger was born.

Even in his forties and fifties, Tin Man still can't accept the fact that real women go to the bathroom (Barbie Benton sure never did!), get food between their teeth, have cellulite, and don't walk around in spike heels when they are relaxing at home.

So many things about real women (that would be you) horrify the Tin Man that it's a miracle he doesn't call 911 when he sees you first thing in the morning.

He may complain that: You kiss too hard, dress too cheap, don't dress cheap enough, wear too much perfume, don't wear enough. And, of course, there's that miserably inconsiderate way you have of, er, getting older.

He will give you a concerned look and say, "Are you happy with that extra weight? Not that it bothers me or anything, I was just wondering if it bothered you."

If the Tin Man does break down and finally utter "I love you," he sounds like he's in the middle of passing a difficult stool.

Don't torture yourself. If you even think, "If only I was prettier, thinner, richer, sexier, younger, cooler, somehow *better*" (fill in the blank), you do yourself a big disservice.

First off, the Tin Man will never want you if you are attainable. He can't want someone who wants him back. He has his memories of a lost love, his ideal, who conveniently disappeared or died (probably of boredom) when he was still in his twenties. This tragedy explains his inability to commit.

This brings us to the big *Who cares?*

Besides, he'll never find you as exciting to look at as he finds himself. Again, who needs the competition? The only good thing is that you'll spend so much time in the plastic surgeon's office, you could run off with the doctor.

CHARACTERISTICS OF THE BREED

Fartsy and not artsy: He's wound so tight that he doesn't even realize that he is taking on old man traits. No? Then explain his addiction to the nature and food channels.

Controlled and controlling: Check out the Jacuzzi with the robes artfully thrown about.

Beware the man who "encourages" you to take up tennis.

Beware the man who has one remote control for his entire TV/stereo system.

GOLDEN RULE #4
If he doesn't make your heart sing now, he never will.

RIGHT SUIT/WRONG MAN #3: SO NICE NO SPICE

He may have been to Armani. He may have a Mercedes or other expensive, flashy car. He's a bachelor but prefers to live in the suburbs. He's often a professional—doctor (gastric not plastic), lawyer (real estate not criminal), or accountant (taxes can be taxing, he says). He may work in greeting card sales, computers, or civil service.

He has all the things you're looking for—and so help you, if he asks you even one more time which movie you want to see, you may have to kill him. Be careful what you wish for next time.

You think it's you, but it's not.

He finds you exciting. Too bad you don't feel the same way about him.

Don't settle.

Yes, it's the nice (well-off) man in the nice suit who is so dull that he makes beige look exciting.

You can't fault him for anything, really. He wants to do what you want to do. In fact, he *has* to do what you want to do since he can't think of anything he'd like to do himself except maybe check what's on Pay-Per-View. See, he's been so busy acquiring a nice portfolio that he hasn't ever done much except go to Club Med, where he also did nothing. The only thing he has going for him is that he—for sure—doesn't have a fatal sexually transmitted disease.

You know that with any encouragement, he'd marry you.

You also know that only on the days where work was so bad you wanted to set the place on fire would you ever *really* consider it.

But still you think sometimes that anyone is better than no one. And that's just what he is to you. Let's face it, he's no fun. And he won't ever be. He will never make you want to own a red teddy. He doesn't make you laugh, and he doesn't make you cry, either. The last time you made love, you were not all there—you were thinking about what you forgot to pick up at the supermarket. So what are you doing with him? It's time you answered that question.

Fear is what you're doing with him. You're worried that if you dump him, now that you're approaching middle age (a term that was anathema to our generation, by the way), maybe no one will ever want you again.

You stay with him because we come from a generation where our youth meant our looks and our looks meant our sexuality and our sexuality meant our validity as women. Get over yourself!

What makes you think that men at our age are that much more desirable than we are? They aren't. An older guy could always get a younger woman—if he had dough, power, and connections that would help her. This is still going on, and he's still so delusional that he truly believes that she'd be just as crazy about him if he were poor. Sure, she'd love him. She'd miss him, but she'd love him.

You could have a younger man too. Maybe you already

have one, or maybe you decided you didn't want one, since you've already raised one.

After all is said and done, if you give into the no spice, that's what you're dooming yourself to. Better to take the chance in the great unknown than to know exactly where your life will be tomorrow—and the next day and the next day . . .

CHARACTERISTICS OF THE BREED

Boring: He believes that Shelley Winters's performance in *The Poseidon Adventure* was perhaps the greatest dramatic performance he's ever seen. He also thinks Kathie Lee Gifford is a dish.

Repressed: He's so inhibited he makes Richard Nixon look like Bill Clinton. The worst thing he's ever done is to bootleg QuickBooks accounting software. He loves the part when the Price Waterhouse guys come out during the Academy Awards.

GOLDEN RULE #5
You *can* settle, but you have to live with the settlement.

WRONG MAN/RIGHT SUIT #4: MR. I'LL TAKE IT

So you haven't had sex in two years. That still doesn't make a man who openly picks his nose, ears, teeth, or toes okay.

There's Mr. Right, Mr. Wrong, and Mr. I'll Take It. Well, don't take it, because you're not that desperate. And even if you are that desperate, don't take it.

He will disappear for hours in the bathroom with a month's supply of *Time* and *Newsweek,* but if you're in there more than three and a half minutes, he'll knock on the door, yelling, "What's going on in there? Didja fall in?"

They should pass legislation forcing him to keep his shoes on twenty-four hours a day. In addition to some very upsetting personal habits, Mr. I'll Take It is so tight he needs 3-In-One oil to walk. Despite this, he has the gall to take you to expensive restaurants and order the most expensive things on the menu. It's not until the bill comes that he thumps his forehead and says, "Jeez! I left my credit cards at home! I guess you'll have to take care of this. Catch you next time." Only the same thing happens the next time.

When he asks you if you've seen your girlfriends naked, he's not conducting an anthropological survey.

You can date Mr. I'll Take It for two years and never meet his kids. Is he trying to protect them or just mortally insult you? Probably both.

In short, the price of having a man like this is much too expensive.

CHARACTERISTICS OF THE BREED

Hygiene: Not a top priority. Tendency to hot dog burp.
Table manners: Table what?

Personal wealth: Who knows, since you haven't ever experienced any of it.

GOLDEN RULE #6
Being the dish on the side is *always* sexier than being the main course. For him.

WRONG MAN/RIGHT SUIT #5: MARRIED WITH (GROWN) CHILDREN

In theory, an affair with a married man should be good for you—as long as you know going in that you probably aren't going to end up going out much with the guy, or even end up with the guy, especially at this stage of the game.

On the upside, it can be a great way for boomer babes to fill in the gaps in our sex lives and get over that dry phase. A fling with a married man gives you an excuse to buy new underwear and lose weight. In a kind of perverse way, a man who is literally unavailable is "safer" than a single man who is emotionally unavailable. Remember that maxim when you are sitting alone on Christmas Eve or Saturday night like crazy Glenn Close in *Fatal Attraction*. After all, it's not that he doesn't *want* to be with you, it's that he *can't*.

You can handle this emotionally only if you're in it:

A. Just for the sex

B. Just for the sex

A SCENARIO THAT GOES BOOMER IN THE NIGHT

There are so many variations on the following story that it's become something like the apocryphal tale of the escaped murderer dressed as a nurse in your house.

Once upon a time, there was a compassionate woman who dated the widower from Larchmont. She couldn't believe her luck that she found such a good one. The widower actually came close to breaking her heart with the sad story of his wife's losing bout with ovarian cancer. Eight months later, she found out that the wife was alive and well and living in Larchmont, ovaries in place.

The girlfriend, who immediately got demoted to the rank of mistress, realizes that she must have been very naive, but *really*, she asks, how could she expect that anyone would make up a story about his wife having cancer? Good question.

The married lover's generic answer about waiting for the kids to grow up is, of course, bogus at this stage of our lives, to say the least. He's too old by now to have little kids from his first marriage, and his new wife, who loves him for himself, is probably only twenty herself.

The truth is that by the time both sets of kids grow up, he's grown old and doesn't want to hand over half of his life savings and pension to an ex-wife.

He should just be honest and say, "Sorry, babe, I just can't leave 'til all the kids are dead." Because he ain't going anywhere, not in this lifetime anyway.

He fully expects that you'll understand that—who knows?—he might get laid off, downsized, or God knows what. He doesn't, after all, want to spend his sunset years in a rooming house with the bathroom down the hall. *You* might end up there, however, if you keep picking lousy men.

CHARACTERISTICS OF THE BREED

Dining habits: Loves restaurants where there is generally one candle to illuminate the whole place. Loves those quaint places where it's just you and him, preferably outside U.S. territorial waters, or at least twenty-five miles from home.

Financial score card: Generally has more money than the average guy (except for the Tin Man), since he's never paid alimony or child support.

Men, Part 3:

Mr. Right's in the Wrong Suit

Before we tell you how to find a great guy, you must swear
to burn Golden Rule #7 into your brain. It is, without a
doubt, the most important of all the golden rules.

No matter what your mother said about companionship,
she was wrong.

Great sex is what makes you stay crazy about someone.

Great sex is what makes you want to be alone with someone rather than plan couple outings. Great sex can overcome almost anything, including being forced to listen to Grateful Dead music.

GOLDEN RULE #8

Screw the conventional wisdom—get 'em while they're hot.

RIGHT MAN/WRONG SUIT #1: JUST SPRUNG

We've been told since birth that a guy needs time to lick his wounds after a breakup. Don't go through his divorce with him, they say. He needs time to regroup himself, we're told.

Yeah? Well, while they're regrouping, there are hordes of hungry women out there ready to pounce. Women who've never dreamed of making—or eating—casseroles learn the art overnight.

Here's what you need to know about Just Sprung: He knows how to be married. He knows how to share. He doesn't hog the covers. He puts the toilet seat down. He calls and asks if you need anything from the store. His side of the bed is not the only one set up for a human. He can talk to your kids like they're people, not pets.

He's used to living with a woman and so is used to the humanity of bodily functions, panty hose, stomach viruses, T-shirts to bed, shoes everywhere, bladder infections, mood swings, makeup in the bedroom, the occasional blood on the sheets, and the fact that women you live with don't wake up in full hair and makeup.

Therefore, the best time for grabbing a good one is within minutes of his split.

CHARACTERISTICS OF THE BREED

Smart: Can help your kids with their science projects. May be a computer whiz and will spend hours teaching you things and retrieving your irretrievably lost documents.

Funny: Really laughs at your jokes. He's comfortable with funny women.

Sexy: Has been in a sexless marriage long enough to know what's important. Is so comfortable with his own sexuality that he's happy to shop for you in Victoria's Secret but is still turned on when you show up for bed in socks and a T-shirt.

Kind: Takes care of you when you're sick. Doesn't worry about getting your germs when you have the flu. Will always be available to pick your kids up from school.

GOLDEN RULE #9
Clothes definitely don't make the man.

RIGHT MAN/WRONG SUIT #2: SHORT-SLEEVE SHIRT

You can't believe you agreed to go to dinner with him, but you find yourself nonetheless sitting in some restaurant with him on a Thursday night. He wears a short-sleeve dress shirt and a tie. He thinks he's dressed up. You didn't even know they still made those shirts, and they probably don't. It's so thin you can see his—yes—undershirt through it. You didn't know anyone still wore undershirts, and they probably don't. He's wearing Sans-A-Belt slacks. You didn't know they made them anymore, and they probably don't. They are blue or brown. He doesn't like to shop, so he may have owned this ensemble since Jesus was a baby.

This may in fact be enough to make you turn tail and run out of the Red Lobster or TGIF he's taken you to. So far, so bad. Then you notice. He smiles and his face lights up. He tells jokes that truly make you laugh. Hard.

Take Lenny the judge. He was a blind date, and he wore terrible blue embossed slacks and a tan short-sleeve shirt. He was a mess. Lucky for Lenny that he wore that robe all day or criminals would have been forced to call the fashion police and have the judge arrested for bad taste.

He was married once and his wife dressed him. They divorced and he never went clothes shopping again. The clothes he bought twenty years before were pure polyester, so short of them melting in a fire, they were good as new for decades.

If Lenny wasn't so funny, he wouldn't have made it past the all-you-can-eat-shrimp phase of the dinner. When the check came, he looked at the bill, then looked back. "Do you fool around," he asked. "No," came the reply. Lenny looked back at the bill and said, "Oh, I see. In that case, you had the creamed spinach and the chicken special. . . ."

The remark was so funny and unexpected that Lenny the

judge got a second, third, and fourth chance. Eventually, he even bought a pair of normal slacks without a built-in belt. The relationship didn't last all that long, but Lenny was a good man and was passed along to a friend who found in him all the things that were hidden under the polyester slacks and short-sleeve dress shirt.

This is a good guy who looks bad. He can improve. His sense of humor makes it worth being with someone whose outfit is humiliating. Take him shopping. He knows how to shop with a woman. Stick to Ralph Lauren. If you make him trendy, he'll still be wearing the same baggy Kenzo pants in the twenty-first century, which will look as nightmarish then as Sans-A-Belts do now.

CHARACTERISTICS OF THE BREED

Smart: He's got a breathtaking scope of knowledge, from rock to politics to movies to restaurants in Provence.

Funny: He can genuinely make you belly laugh.

Sexy: How did someone who looks like that learn to do this? Good question. He's the ultimate unselfish man.

Kind: He genuinely cares when your kids, your mother, your best friends get sick.

GOLDEN RULE #10

A man who's his own man knows how to make a woman feel like a natural woman.

RIGHT MAN/WRONG SUIT #3: THE MAN IN THE GOLD TOURINO

As they say on pizza boxes, you've tried the rest, now try the best.

The Man in the Gold Tourino isn't someone you'd ever expect to end up with. He's not your type. He's pushy. He's tasteless. He dresses like he thinks Steven Seagal should. He drives a huge car. He plays poker with his friends instead of attending art openings.

He's also hilarious, sexy, and his own man. He's worth it. What makes it all worth it is that he's everything we all thought we would be in the sixties: a total nonconformist who works within the confines of the real world. Just generally not for anyone else.

He's tough, but not with you. In fact, he's the guy you can go into the worst neighborhoods with and never feel scared. And you should get used to it, because he knows that the best restaurants are always in the worst neighborhoods.

Spotting the elusive gem: First off, he doesn't care what he's wearing. You might find him wearing something so frightening that even your mother, who wants you to get married, would turn away in horror. Think net shirts, loud Hawaiian shirts, cut-off sweatshirts, insane workout wear. He has muscles sticking out of that truly terrible Van Heusen shirt. And a big chest.

His hair: There is only one word to describe it: *Oy*, as they say in France. Think ponytail.

He thinks a seafood fork is for salad, steak tartare is in, and prefers a good diner to a "fine" restaurant.

He's more likely to own a couple of bowling alleys than a bank.

He's tough as nails, but he's a secret romantic. If you don't tell anyone, he will send you flowers. The flowers will be stuck in green Styrofoam, have flat backs, and lots of ferns. They look like miniature funeral arrangements. He means well.

He's unpretentious, he's underrated, he's a diamond in the very rough. He's a real guy, who's adorable, sexy, funny.

Hey, you can always take him to a hairdresser—after you've known him for a decade or so. If you try it sooner than that, he will freak that you are trying to change him and get in his tasteless car and drive away at the speed of light.

Remember, we always wanted a nonconformist—it's just that it was supposed to be a nonconformist who was tortured and miserable. That was then, and for God's sake, this is now.

CHARACTERISTICS OF THE BREED

Smart: He will shock you with what he knows. It just doesn't show.

Funny: He is among the funnier people you will ever know. He sees life as everyone else wishes they could. He, blessedly, can laugh at himself. He'll even teach you to laugh at yourself.

Sexy: Yes. This is the genuine article. He makes all the others who came before him look like Don Knotts.

Kind: He, too, genuinely cares when your kids, your mother, and your best friend get sick. He drives you and your family places. Wouldn't dream of bad-mouthing his ex-wife or girlfriends. He works for himself but is happy to share the spoils with you. He is not beyond spontaneously buying you shoes.

GOLDEN RULE #11
Boomer babes were born to break the rules. What's good for the gander is good for the goose.

RIGHT MAN/WRONG SUIT #4: YOUNGER THAN SPRINGTIME

When nineteen-year-old Oona O'Neill married sixty-year-old Charlie Chaplin, her dad thought she was taking a Long Day's Journey into Old Goatdom.

Who can ever forget "The Killer," Jerry Lee Lewis. He married his thirteen-year-old cousin. She unfortunately did not outlive her much older husband.

Hey, if he can do it, then we can too. We are not, of course, talking about marrying a nineteen year old, murdering him, or even having him mysteriously disappear. We are talking about taking on a younger lover.

What was traditionally deemed unacceptable is now out

of the closet and into the bed. We boomer babes have not only taken what was traditionally a guy's turf—his job, his salary, and his gym—and made them our own, we've now moved in on his first line of defense against middle age—younger lovers.

He's here, he's young, he's fun, and screw the consequences.

For one thing, when you open yourself up to younger men, you open up the available manpower substantially, even exponentially.

And we do it better than our male counterparts ever did. Here's the deal with older men and younger women: He's always rich and she's always gorgeous. Let's face it, you never see a rich older man with an ugly younger woman, or a hot-looking young woman with a poor older man. The same can't be said about us. It's sort of like the way Americans invented TV and the Japanese improved on it.

We took the basic idea and made it better. We stripped away the mandatory requirements of wealth and beauty on both sides. Chances are good that if you're in it, you're in it because he's more fun for you, and you're more interesting for him than people your own ages.

He's tired of yuppies in suits and sneakers, and you're tired of listening to "Stairway to Heaven."

He was brought up in a more liberated era so he's not stuck with the traditional concepts of what a woman *should* be and *should* look like. You like him for that—he's not damaged goods. And by the time he hits his male midlife crisis and looks for a younger woman, you'll already have Alzheimer's.

A younger man is like a hit of estrogen without bothering to visit the gynecologist. Enjoy it. It's great—as long as you don't start obsessing about your *own* age. You know what? Your age doesn't bother the younger man. It bothers men our own age more. After all, Younger than Springtime is not worrying about getting older.

But, like every other relationship, this one has its downside, and it's a ticking time bomb: At some point, he will probably want kids. Kids? You'd let him play with yours, but they are his age!

Then there's his mother. She'll probably look at you with disdain and horror, his friends may call you the poor man's Cher. Fortunately you're beyond caring about that nonsense by now. Unfortunately, he probably isn't.

But since when does life come with a hang tag guarantee? If it did, we would have returned a lot of those earlier losers a lot sooner.

Jump in, have fun, don't make him your life's work, and remember that we started the whole cool thing, and you'll be fine.

CHARACTERISTICS OF THE BREED

Smart: He's smart in ways you probably aren't. He can install the CD-ROM in your computer and actually knows what it's for. He will update your taste in rock by at least twenty years.

Funny: Well, you can't have everything. He probably will laugh at things that leave you cold.

Sexy: He has at least as much energy as you.

Kind: His mother taught him that John Wayne was a jerk, so he's considerate to women and doesn't equate sensitivity with effemininity.

GOLDEN RULE # EVEN DOZEN
To an older man, you're always a younger woman he's grateful to have.

RIGHT MAN/WRONG SUIT #5: OLDY NOT MOLDY

There's a lot to be said for older men, too. For one thing, you will always be young to him.

More important, he's settled in and isn't about to run off looking for himself. And he will never, and we repeat *never,* utter the following words: "ciao," "empower," "yo," "enjoy," or "disingenuous." He doesn't believe he has lived before in *any* form. He will never discuss *The Celestine Prophesy.* He doesn't know who Barney is, and if he did, he wouldn't care unless he has some kind of licensing agreement or something.

He likes to travel and likes to spend money. He likes to have a good time and likes to have a good time with you.

He's also experienced—very—and is old enough to know

that pleasing a woman is a lot of fun. He is happy to spend days in bed having sex, since he's got the time.

You know by now that getting older means avoiding being on top at all costs. (If you don't know what we're talking about, put a hand mirror on a table and look down into it. You'll understand right away.)

The beauty of being with an older man is that you can be in any position in bed, any time of the day, and you'll still look young to him. Cheaper than a surgeon and a lot more fun.

Like the younger man, this relationship too has its built-in time bomb: death. *You* may die from all that activity.

Of course, we aren't talking about an age span like the one between Anna Nicole Smith, who claimed to be twenty-eight when she married a ninety-year-old billionaire. Those sixty-two-year age spans just never work. And, poor thing, after she went and wore her wedding gown to his funeral and all, his family still snookered her out of his money. Good thing she loved him just for himself.

We're talking about a ten-, fifteen-, even twenty-year age span. If you fall in love, have a good time. You know going in that at some point he'll probably get infirm, but then again, he may not. Besides, it's better than growing old with your first husband who was already old at twenty-six.

CHARACTERISTICS OF THE BREED

Smart: He gives real estate advice, stock tips, tax tips, and free investment counseling. He actually seems to know what tax-deferred split mutual funds are. He will patiently explain it all to you, until you actually understand it.

Funny: At last, a man who has a working knowledge of all thirty-nine episodes of *The Honeymooners.* He will never want to go to a Pauley Shore movie, watch *Friends,* or see anything involving Andrew Dice Clay.

Sexy: Sex is better, better, and better. For one thing, he is totally into pleasing you, because he feels lucky to have you and has had enough women in his time to know the difference between regular sex and passionate in-love sex.

Kind: He's more tolerant. If you make a mistake, he considers himself a teacher, not a disciplinarian who gets annoyed that you aren't Madonna/Madonna. He's not a big baby like so many baby boomer men.

He's seen a lot of life, and that's made him more compassionate.

When you tell an older guy for the first time that you love him, you can be sure he'll be thrilled instead of freaked out. He'll tell you he loves you back—if he hasn't already done so. He knows life's too short for games. Besides, he's already won the jackpot, and that, by the way, would be you.

e i g h t

M e n ,   P a r t   4 :

H o w   t o   M e e t   a   G u y

> **GOLDEN RULE #13**
> **Put down the remote, get off the couch, and get out of the house.**

Now for the good news: It's finally the nineties, and men are back! Despite rumors of their scarcity, men—tall ones, short ones, cute ones, funny ones, just flat-out good ones—are plentiful. This crop has been ripening on the vine for years.

They're the guys we overlooked in our twenties and be-friended in our thirties. These are the guys who never af-

fected a full Berman and had no interest in being profes-
sionally good-looking. Where have they been? They were
busy. They were out of control in their thirties, got scared by
it in their forties, and are ripe for the picking in their fifties.

Like us, they've been in and out of relationships—looking
for love in all the right places, finding all the wrong people,
and not knowing when to hit the road.

So how do you find these gems? Take off the blinders
and stop looking for him anywhere "singles" congregate.
He'd rather die. If he *is* there, it's because he hasn't left his
wife yet.

Now how do you find him?

Hard as it may be to believe, if the perfect man hasn't
somehow wandered into your living room by mistake in the
past fifty years, chances are good he won't be showing up
anytime soon, either. Therefore, you gotta get up off your
keister and get out there.

Somewhere around 50 percent of Americans meet their
spouses at work. Therefore, you won't meet a date if you
work, say, for a gynecologist, but you will if you *are* a gynecologist. See, working in an OB/GYN's office will put you
in touch only with other women. But if you're an OB/GYN,
you will meet tons of other doctors, many of whom are male.

Jobs that require business travel are also great for meeting men. Planes, by the way, are the greatest place on earth
to meet guys. Well, off the earth, at any rate.

So if you work at a lady farm (women's magazine, cosmetics company, NOW, fashion industry, women's bou-

tique), you probably have as much chance of meeting a guy as staying home on your couch at night.

Should you quit if you work in a place that's mostly women, or in a place that you've worked forever and have never met a guy? Well, yes, actually. But not until you've found another job.

What jobs are loaded with men? Newspapers, TV stations, construction companies, government agencies, sanitation departments, fire departments, you get the picture.

MEETING MEN OUTSIDE THE OFFICE

If you know in your heart that men who place personals, answer personals, hang out in singles' bars, attend singles' functions, and make dates in cyberspace are not for you, then why in hell would you subject yourself to personal ads, singles' bars, singles' functions, and virtual flirting in chat rooms?

What we're trying to say is simple: *Don't even go there.*

You're at the stage where you know for sure what you enjoy doing. Wouldn't it be nice to find a guy who really likes those kinds of things, too?

You like politics? Join the local political club.

You like cooking? Lots of guys are in cooking classes these days.

Drink too much? AA meetings are like unpaid marriage brokers.

Guilty? Volunteer in a soup kitchen. (We're not saying to

marry a homeless guy, we're saying that P/C guys with consciences volunteer there!)

Computer nerd? Go to computer conventions.

Obsessed with Roswell? Attend UFO spotting conventions.

Like to run? Join the Road Runners Club.

Have Hollywood aspirations? So does every guy in North America. Sign up for a screenwriting course.

Worried about money? Take an investments class.

Have a friend you can trust? Ask the friend if she/he has a friend.

Just always remember the immortal words of The Supremes, "You can't hurry love" and then—get off the couch!

nine

They're Even Older Than *We* Are!

- Tina Turner, 58
- Goldie Hawn, 52
- Candice Bergen, 52
- Deborah Harry, 53
- Britt Ekland, 56
- Martha Stewart, 55
- Cher, 52
- Michelle Phillips, 54
- Raquel Welch, 58
- Sophia Loren, 64

- Joan Baez, 57
- Ali MacGraw, 60
- Carmen (model), 67
- Susan Sarandon, 52
- Ann-Margret, 57
- Dixie Carter, 59
- Carly Simon, 52
- Diana Ross, 54
- Gloria Steinem, 62
- Mia Farrow, 53
- Lauren Hutton, 55
- Bette Midler, 53
- Farrah Fawcett, 52
- Linda Evans, 55
- Priscilla Presley, 53
- Jane Fonda, 61
- Faye Dunaway, 57
- Suzanne Somers, 52
- Marlo Thomas, 59
- Shelley Fabares, 54
- Catherine Deneuve, 55
- Patti Smith, 51

"We've Taken Over the President's Office"

When Mark Rudd said this at Columbia University in 1969, it meant they'd booted university president Grayson Kirk out of his cushy office. Students sat at his desk and smoked his cigars. Twenty-three years later, when all the rest of us said, "We've taken over the president's office," we meant we'd taken over *the* president's office. In Washington. By election.

We (as in all boomer babies) have also, come to think of it, taken over, and in some cases overrun:

- Corporations
- Alcoholics Anonymous
- Gyms
- Multinational conglomerates
- Hollywood
- Ashrams
- University faculties
- Upscale rehabs
- Mutual fund markets
- Golf courses
- Spas
- TV
- Politics
- Radio (talk shows)
- Weight Watchers

WE'VE SPAWNED . . .

There are so many of us that the sheer size and brattiness of our mass meant that whole industries, not to mention support groups, came into existence simply because we did. In fact, there are so many twelve-step programs now that you need a StairMaster just to get through them.

We also spawned:

- Cocaine Anonymous
- Sex Anonymous
- Overeaters Anonymous

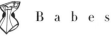

- Anonymous Anonymous
- Frozen yogurt
- Cult deprogrammers
- Actor Scientologists
- Deadheads
- Elvis spotters
- Elvis impersonators
- Jim Morrison Is Alive clubs
- Las Vegas as a cheesy family resort
- Blow dryers
- Leather after forty
- Motorcycles after fifty
- Nail salons
- Meditation instead of medication
- Motivational speakers
- Infomercials (by people who couldn't make it as motivational speakers)
- Hugely expensive rock concerts (as opposed to rock and roll shows featuring fifty-three groups)
- Plastic boobs in a bag
- Plastic lips
- Millionaire plastic surgeons
- Chicago, the group that wouldn't die (unlike rockers with actual talent)
- Sixties revivals
- Seventies revivals
- Charles Manson

- More Kennedys
- Bill Clinton
- Generation X'ers (who have a greater sense of entitlement than we did—if at all possible)

eleven

From a Vision to the Invisible Woman

Age is a case of mind over matter. If you don't mind,
it doesn't matter.
—Mark Twain

Have you noticed a disturbing new phenomenon over the last few years? Now, when you walk past a pack of construction workers—a group you always considered snorting, slobbering adolescents—they act as if Gertrude Stein just walked by.

Welcome to the ranks of the new invisible woman.

Some other signs of this phenomenon: That man you thought was giving you the eye in that restaurant was actually looking to see if you ordered the special. You're shocked that your young coworkers think of you as someone from their parents' generation, even though you are. You have the sickening realization that the last time a clerk called you "miss" instead of "ma'am" was during Ronald Reagan's first term of office.

What's going on here?

How is it possible that we are almost the same age as the president of the United States? How did postal workers, dentists, stockbrokers, and even the butcher get to be younger than us? How did we get to be this old and, more to the point, how come we don't look young anymore?

Now the big question as middle age rears its jowls is: What do you strut when your stuff has stopped?

The answer is simple, really. It's your brave, experienced-but-not-bitter stuff that is the beauty—yes, beauty—of aging. We came of age in the most exciting of times and had a greater impact on society than any other generation before us. So who among us would trade that experience along with our hard-won confidence and interesting lives for our twenty-something bodies fraught with insecurity and lousy taste in men? (Okay, you in the back row, sit down!)

We boomer babes are the swell of the population, what has been called "the pig in the python," so we get to make the rules and break the rules as we crawl along. So now it's time to make some new rules and dispel some old myths about middle-aged women, women who are supposed to become invisible because they are no longer visions of youth. The times are a-changing once again.

We're not saying that aging doesn't stink. It does. It's not easy to wake up one morning, look in the mirror, and realize that even though you had gone to bed with a perfectly functioning pair of lips, they had disappeared!

All right, we won't try to tell you that the sight of your first chin hair isn't an unnerving moment. How can we, really, when the offending hair can be seen for a three-mile radius? In fact, the truly wretched among us may be afflicted with what has been vulgarly referred to as "fur face," a downy expanse of facial hair. Fortunately, "fur face" can be detected only when the sun lies directly overhead. And while we're at it, let's mention that we don't exactly look like we looked in 1974 in a bikini, either.

Life's a trade-off, and for all the things that you lose (lips) and gain (hips), you should remember that—if you do it right—aging brings strength, *real* strength. And strength is sexy.

Here we are again, breaking another rule and breaking down another barrier: It's up to us to overthrow the invisible woman. There's no better way to stay visible than to believe in yourself and exercise your strength.

So how do you go about doing this?

First, read this book.

Second, lose—once and for all—that Donna Reed eager-to-please, good-girl mentality.

In short: Grow up—a very different thing from growing old. It means simply to get out of high school. If any of the following sound disturbingly familiar to you—please, it's been thirty years. Graduate, already:

- You actually wait by the phone for some schmo who doesn't call. (This means you're still suffering from pre-prom trauma; you really need to get past this.)
- You believe that people with more than you are better than you.
- Approval is still more important than anything.
- Life is not complete without a boyfriend.
- You look at the company you work for as your high school. The only problem is that the blind loyalty you give your corporation is misplaced since, unlike schools, they're in it for the money. So it's a big shock when you get expelled, or rather, downsized.
- The happiest people are the popular people.
- The ideal to strive for is to be the other (lesser) half of a couple. And you keep yourself in miserable marriages and unhappy relationships for the sake of this ideal.
- Your best friend falls in love and begins a great new relationship. Instead of being happy for her, you feel abandoned. Worse, you feel jealous. Please! You're fifty, not fifteen. Do you phone people— ex-boyfriend, ex-girlfriend, ex-boss, ex-relative— then hang up when they answer? Stop! You're not a kid and besides, these days there's Caller ID. This means you can get busted and be exposed as a disgruntled fifty-year-old making crank calls.
- You start a lot of sentences with "If only . . ."

It's ideas like these that will keep you forever waiting, cloaked in good-girl misery, looking at life from the outside. Now is the time to graduate into a whole new world. Now is the time to tell anyone who refuses to respect you and your boundaries in a clear, proud voice, "Blow it out your ass!"

twelve

Menopause: Hers — Is It Hot in Here or Is It Just Me?

You've read all the articles, now live the experience! Boomer babes have an uncontrollable need to talk about themselves, so when we approached this midlife marker, menopause burst out of the closet quicker than a hot flash at a business meeting.

The "change," as your mother used to call it, is, no matter what they say, a big pain in the ass. It isn't a wonderful thing, despite those women's books that call for you to join your friends in the woods, bang tribal drums, wear big jewelry, and bray native chants while celebrating the "pause." Oy.

What it comes down to is this: You spent the last thirty-five or so years complaining about your period; now you'll spend the next few years complaining about its passing.

But, given boomer babes' history, it won't be mindless complaining. This is the generation that demanded that fathers be let into the delivery room and that began monitoring their own pregnancies.

The "change" is about to change. For one thing, 35 million women in the United States alone—900 million worldwide—will enter menopause in the next fifteen years. God only knows what the effect of 900 billion hot flashes will be on global warming.

Happily, there are so many of us that we're taking menopause out of the closet for the first time, exchanging tales of the sweats and the fear and loathing of fur face.

First, let's state the obvious. Menopause is not, repeat *not*, a disease. It's the beginning of the next third of your life. It's only in this century that the majority of women live past menopause, so this last third of your life is actually a bonus.

It's up to us to trash the image of menopausal women as cranky, dried up, unattractive, and about as sexy as Edith Bunker.

Instead, we're embarking on a new phase of life, a phase where, incidentally, we will never have PMS or menstrual cramps, run out of tampons, and never ever have to worry about getting pregnant. Isn't that liberating?

Speaking of liberating, it's interesting to note that in cultures where older women gain social freedom and are elevated with age—Japan, India, Thailand—there are absolutely no symptoms of menopause. While Americans have always been fixated on youth, in China age is revered. So not surprisingly, there isn't even a Chinese word for "hot flash."

If you've defined yourself either by your looks alone, or by being a mom, menopause is not going to be a walk, pardon the expression, in the woods for you.

If you haven't started menopause yet, you should start thinking about it. If it's just starting, you can expect to find none (20 percent of all women experience no menopausal symptoms), some, or all of the following: irregular periods, hot flashes (or to be strictly PC, "power surges"), anxiety, flaky skin, vaginal dryness, sagging breasts, and, heaven help us, incontinence. Oh, the horror of laughing coquettishly and wetting your pants!

If all this isn't bad enough, the stress that today's generation of women experiences can make some of these symptoms even more intense. If you let it, that is.

Because boomers are so vocal about menopause (and everything else, for that matter), the medical profession has steadily been building a big business: the menopause industry. There are pills, patches, creams, and implants as well as tests that measure your hormone level and your bone density.

It may be overkill, but it's a major improvement over the traditional treatment of menopause. Doctors (male) would listen, nod their heads sympathetically, and then write out a prescription for tranquilizers.

THE HOT FLASH AND OTHER FLASHES OF INSPIRATION

While hot flashes are not exactly hazardous to your health, they are as image-enhancing as splitting your pants.

Flashes are defined by medical journals as "sudden, inappropriate excitation of heat-release mechanisms." Inappropriate, no kidding.

Note: You babes who are bored with all the hype and hysteria surrounding menopause and just want to go with the flow, or rather with the no-flow, good for you. You must have been a tomboy, or at least a WASP, but at any rate, you don't have to be told to keep exercising (like you'd ever stop).

Besides stripping down to your bra and finding an open window, there are lots and lots of things you can do to handle hot flashes and all the other symptoms of menopause.

EXERCISE

Even if you do nothing else, you must exercise. It's the best thing you can do to fight the effects of aging and menopause. Regular exercise helps maintain weight and energy while reducing the risk of heart disease, diabetes, high blood pressure, and that dreaded curse of the older woman—osteoporosis. If you're worried about wrinkles, think of how you'd feel shrinking to a four-feet, nine-inch crone with a dowager's hump!

Here's the part you might hate: In order to maintain a reasonable facsimile of your average before-menopause weight, you must, repeat, *must,* include aerobics as part of your daily life. Walking, biking, running, dancing, tennis, and swimming—take your pick—must be a part of every exercise regime. See Chapter 15, "A Babe's Guide to Torture (aka Exercise)."

HRT (HORMONE REPLACEMENT THERAPY) AKA ERT (ESTROGEN REPLACEMENT THERAPY)

These days, the majority of gynecologists are in favor of HRT, provided that there is no history of breast cancer in your immediate family. Right now about 28 percent of all women over forty-five who are menopausal take HRT. It reduces the risk of cardiovascular disease, osteoporosis, and Alzheimer's while zapping hot flashes and improving muscle tone. Thank you, Lord, it also relieves vaginal dryness and is great for your skin. Here's a bonus: If you score HRT, your future may be free of that plaintive cry, "I've fallen and I can't get up."

Of course, there's that ever-present female fear—the same fear that made you afraid to give up smokes—weight gain. The acronym HRT doesn't mean Hefty Rotund Tub, so forget the fear you will look like a chicken plumped up on hormones. The experts *swear* that any weight gain that comes with HRT is probably due to dramatic metabolism changes that occur during menopause. Like it or not.

So if your idea of a *real* medical crisis is being weighed in at your doctor's office, there is only one solution: Eat less and exercise more.

When you begin HRT, work out the dosage that's best for you with your gyno. The most common is combination therapy: estrogen in the form of Premarin (who cares if it's made from the urine of pregnant mares?) along with Provera (synthetic progestin), which reduces the risk of uterine cancer. We asked Jane Galasso, M.D., a gynecologist in New York City, how long she would recommend women staying on HRT, and her answer was simple: "We believe forever."

Some other methods of HRT are progesterone without estrogen, transdermal estrogen patch, birth control pills (they're baaack, and yes, they have estrogen).

VITAMIN THERAPY

You can use vitamin therapy with or without HRT. Here, then, is a starter kit: vitamin E (400–1,000 IU) relieves night sweats, hot flashes, backaches, fatigue, insomnia, and heart palpitations; vitamin D (400 IU); vitamins B_5 and B_6 (400 mg); vitamin C (500–2,000 mg).

You also need lecithin (1 capsule, helps emulsify the vitamin E) and calcium (1,000–1,500 mg a day, the higher amount if you're not on HRT). You can get enough calcium in three glasses of skim milk. If you're really virtuous, you can eat lots and lots of broccoli. Or you can use calcium supplements. Calcium citrate is absorbed most readily, followed by calcium carbonate found in oyster shell supplements and antacids. You can also chew two Tums each day to get your calcium hit.

HERBAL REMEDIES

Dr. Tso Nam Chan of the UN Acupuncture Center in New York City recommends the herbal formula ME-523, which reduces menopausal symptoms and regulates your *chi*. Suffice it to say that sluggish *chi* cramps your style. This tablet contains ginseng, licorice, rhubarb, cinnamon, clove atractylodes, tang-kuei, canidium, coptis, scute, saussurca, and areca seed. Take the herbal remedy in conjunction with an acupuncture treatment designed for menopause.

The most popular herb in menopause treatment is the Chinese herb Dong Quai, which, despite its masculine-sounding name, contains plant estrogens. Dong Quai is available in health food stores and is especially recommended for menopause. Why there is Dong Quai if there is no such thing as a hot flash in China remains a big mystery.

Some of the following herbs are commonly prescribed and, in our opinion, their names alone make them worth trying: unicorn root, evening primrose oil, licorice root, passion flower, chaste berry, angus cactus, chamomile milk thistle, and Siberian ginseng. Less euphonious sounding but equally effective herbs include catnip, hops, and wild turnips.

You can also try dace tea, a mixture of sage, blue vervain, motherwort, blessed thistle, rosemary, and ginseng.

Wild Mexican yam (trade name Pro-gest) is a topically applied natural progesterone that comes in a moisturizing cream or oil. And slippery elm is a vaginal gel applied topically. The mind reels.

ON A PERSONAL NOTE . . .
KEGEL EXERCISES

If you were ever pregnant, you'll remember this from your Lamaze book. Kegel exercises are simple and you can do them anytime, anyplace, without anyone finding out.

Squeeze the sphincter muscles in your pelvic area, count to three, and relax. Do these exercises whenever you can because they are effective in preventing urinary and bladder problems (that is to say, leaking).

But more important, they help keep the muscles around your internal organs tight, which will prevent fallen organs (yikes!) when you're really old and living in that retirement commune. (We came of age in 'em, and we hope we'll come of old age in 'em—communes, that is!)

VAGINAL LUBRICANTS

Doctors recommend the following for vaginal dryness: Astrodglide (this is a vaginal lubricant, not the power steering on a '55 Buick), K-Y jelly (who was the K and who was the Y?), Replens, Lubrin, Maxilube, Transilube (*this* must be the steering on a '55 Buick), vitamin E oil, and Ortho Personal Lubricant.

Do not use petroleum jelly (Vaseline, to you), since it coats the tissues and spreads bacteria. However, God did create petroleum jelly for a reason, and this is definitely one of them: If you smear a bit on your face before you take a shower, you will not dry up. Doris Day, who knows a thing or two about aging, uses it as a night cream. (Some cynics crudely suggest she used it as a camera gel as well).

Also do not use estrogen creams. One study shows that some male partners experience an increase in breast size. Probably the ones who did call the next day—to see if you have an extra bra to spare.

YOGA

In addition to relieving menopausal symptoms and eliminating stress, yoga strengthens the mind and the body. Just take a look at Raquel Welch; she's even older than we are!

BIOFEEDBACK, MEDITATION, VISUALIZATION, AND ACUPUNCTURE

You should check them out if for no other reason than, well, it's your obligation. After all, we came of age listening to the Beatles sing about transcendental meditation!

DON'T SMOKE

Despite the fact that inhaling burning leaves is really fun, and oddly satisfying, it really stinks on every level, and your body doesn't need any more help in aging. Smoking makes you wrinkle faster and causes those awful lines around your lips that make you look like your lips are bleeding when you wear lipstick. And your teeth turn yellow and look like they belong on old farmers.

May we beg you one favor, though: Please don't turn into one of those annoying people who yell and flutter their hands when other people are smoking in the same universe. If nothing else, this ages you faster than smoking a carton a day, at least in perception.

DIET

Unfortunately, the basic rules still apply: You won't get fat if you don't eat like a fatso. More important, you won't be thin if you think like a fatso. See Chapter 14, "A Babe's Guide to Deprivation (aka Diet)."

Fat aside, food and drinks you blithely indulged in over the years can now wreak havoc on your new menopausal self.

YOU MUST CUT BACK ON THE FOLLOWING

- Refined sugar and refined (read: white) flour
- Alcohol
- Caffeine
- Carbonated sodas, including diet sodas
- Fast food
- Chocolate
- Salt
- Spicy foods (you're sweating enough)
- Smoked and processed foods

EAT A LOT OF THE FOLLOWING

Plant estrogens can be found in many plant foods, which are essential to menopausal women. Foods rich in estrogen include:

- Apples
- Alfalfa sprouts
- Split peas
- Spinach
- Especially great: soybean products and linseed

Radical dieting isn't great no matter what age but especially at menopause when you need your vitamin and mineral reserves more than ever.

What it all comes down to is that we must believe that love, sex, and a good quickie are still in the cards for any of us after the age of forty-five. What else on this earth could explain the success of the best-seller *The Bridges of Madison County* (aka *The Bridgework of Madison County*)?

MENOPAUSAL DANGER SIGNALS

- You have your first hot flash, which is about as welcome as a belch at the ballet.
- You suddenly get the urge to do what Farrah did: Take your clothes off as often as possible in front of the greatest number of people, while putting clay all over yourself.
- You haven't lived until you've had a three-period month, followed the next month by a one-tampon period.
- You've taken to wearing the Wonder Bra, which is about as comfortable as having an eight-hour mammogram.
- You honestly believe that if you lose enough weight, your jowls will disappear.
- Compliments that you now accept include the dreaded "interesting," "attractive," and any other adjectives that could have applied to Deborah Kerr at fifty. (No one has ever called Sophia Loren "attractive.")

- Your feet have suddenly taken on an uncanny resemblance to used bricks.
- Your toenails are beginning to look like you picked them up at Jurassic Park.
- You look at your hands and try to convince yourself that the recent liver-colored mark is actually a darling new freckle.
- The only thing slower than your metabolism is the mail with your child-support check in it.
- Alan Alda is starting to look good to you.
- You go to get remarried and realize there's not enough room on the marriage license to list all your exes.
- You've been married to your husband so long you remember when he didn't have hair in his ears.

Menopause: His — Women Are
from Mars, Men Are from Penis

*It's not the men in my life, it's the life in my men
that counts.*
—Mae West

Yes, it happens. They don't talk about it, but it happens. You don't see it in their magazines. They don't talk about it even when it's happening to them—especially when it's happening to them. Male menopause. The pause that doesn't refresh.

Okay, so they can still reproduce; that's nature's way of assuring propagation of the species. But they have hormonal changes all the same. Male menopause—too often like marriage—manifests itself in diminished sexual desire, impotence, nervousness, anxiety, mood changes, and headaches.

It also results in the loss of lean muscle mass. Lastly, male menopause decreases sperm production, although you'd never know it by looking at all those old guys pushing strollers instead of their own walkers.

We said earlier that women who have spent a lifetime living off their looks have the hardest time with menopause. Well, men whose selves and potency are wrapped up in competitiveness, success, and power have the hardest (pardon the expression) time with the psychological effects of male menopause.

Throw into this mix a fragile economy and yuppies biting at their heels, and suddenly the term "downsizing" takes on a new meaning. To make matters worse for guys, by the time they hit fifty they have a 20 percent risk of developing an enlarged prostate, a risk that goes up to 50 percent by the time they hit sixty. Let's face it, as awful as a visit to the gynecologist can be, it's gotta beat visiting your local proctologist.

Perhaps Groucho Marx summed up the plight of the menopausal male best, when he left a poker game saying, "So long, fellas. I guess I'll go upstairs now and see if I can bend one in."

Given that, maybe you shouldn't feel so bad if you've got the beginnings of a beard. How would you like it if you were a guy and lost the hair on your head and found it instead sprouting in your ears and out your nose?

There's all sorts of help available for the menopausal man, as well: testosterone, growth hormones, penile implants, an herb called yohimbine, or the over-the-counter natural sex hormone DHEA. And soon some of the great male minds of medicine will be introducing impotency drugs going by the names of Viagra, Spontane, Vasomex. On top of this there will be a line of suppositories, vacuum pumps, and penile injections. Ouch!

Of course, there's always the common, time-honored antidote to male aging: a young girlfriend. A teenage tootsie is only the beginning.

Capping women's historical and hysterical fear and loathing of aging, you'll be satisfied to know that sales of men's hair coloring have tripled in the last ten years. Rugs, face lifts, face peels, eye lifts, liposuction, baldness pills, bronzers, and back waxing are all rising faster than, well, faster than let's call it their libidos.

We're especially horrified by the brisk sales of a somewhat newer item: the Super Shaper Briefs. No, this is not a Wonder Jock, but a Wonder Butt. According to their manufacturer, Rush Industries, they give you eye-catching buttocks instantly.

See, the terrible truth is that men's butts do a slow dissolve and can be practically nonexistent once they hit the big M.

The case of the disappearing butt is often accompanied by disappearing calves. The reason? As guys lose testosterone, they're left with their supply of estrogen. (Why our legs never got thin from too much estrogen remains a miserable mystery.) And eventually their breasts grow too, another miserable mystery of life you are not entitled to.

What follows is a list of some of the alarming side effects of male menopause (male midlife crisis). These symptoms can strike your man, your next-door-neighbor, your coworkers, and the guy at the deli counter. Who knows, even Eric Clapton may not be immune! Actually, come to think of it, except for his one date with Cher, most of his girlfriends look so young they must think *Blind Faith* is only a Robert Ulrich TV movie and *Cream* is a fattening dairy product.

MIDLIFE DANGER SIGNALS

- He joins the Hair Club for Men and comes home from his first session wearing what appears to be a live farm animal on his head.
- He finds and actually attempts to fit into his Sgt. Pepper's Lonely Hearts Club Band jacket that made him look like such a rebel only—what—thirty years ago!
- When he talks about dating an "older woman," he's actually referring to someone who's two years *younger* than he is.
- He tells you he's taken up a sport and comes home with his clothes still pressed in his gym bag. Either there's an on-site Chinese laundry at that gym or he's been working out with a live dumbbell. Man your battle stations.
- He joins a gym (really this time), loses weight, goes vegetarian, starts listening to New Age music while

discussing "wellness issues," and begins to believe that attractive young women are flirting with him everywhere he goes.

- He buys Just for Men hair dye and thinks people will believe that he always had beige hair.
- He gets tickets to a Pearl Jam concert and believes he passes for someone who should be there.
- He takes to wearing Lycra bike shorts, effectively advancing the cause of trusses into the twenty-first century.
- He dates women who weren't born when JFK—or even JR—was shot.

Menopause, whether it's female or male, is a wake-up call that you're onto the final third of your life. The good thing is that all things are possible, with the possible exception of becoming an Olympic gymnast, at this stage of the game.

fourteen

A Babe's Guide to Deprivation
(aka Diet)

Let's get something straight. Food is one of life's great pleasures. If it wasn't meant to be enjoyed, everything would
taste like sweat socks. If you're going to deny yourself the
pleasures of eating, you might as well put on a hair shirt, go
out into the desert, and hit yourself with chains.

Life's a banquet—just don't go at it like Henry VIII.

How is it that people in European cultures, who seem to
eat for a living, stay trim? Could it be perhaps that they
enjoy food rather than obsess about it?

Writer Laura Fraser recently related this anecdote in a

magazine about an Italian chef caught in the temporary clutches of a professional American dieter. Seems that this woman was taking a cooking class in Tuscany and asked the chef to teach them to make bruschetta *without* olive oil. The chef shrank back in horror but obliged the woman by piling the bread up with tomatoes. "But the thing that made me mad," said the chef, "was that as soon as her friends left the room, *la Signora Dieta* came back into the kitchen and secretly ate six bruschette with olive oil." *La Signora Dieta* turned out to be that doyenne of dieting, Jenny Craig.

Food, to American women, anyway, is like loving a rotten man—we hate ourselves every time we enjoy ourselves. The lesson to be learned, if any, is to indulge in what's good for you and enjoy the forbidden every now and again.

That said, one third of Americans are overweight. Despite everything we've seen, heard, read, and prayed for since we were little girls, there is no miracle way to be thin and eat as much as you want.

Generally, crash, fad, and liquid diets make you fatter in the end, because they trick your body into thinking it's starving, which it is, actually. So when you go off them, your body holds onto the calories to stave off starvation again.

If Jean Harris hadn't killed diet doctor Herman Tarnower, one of us would have for sure.

Besides, it's no longer chic to be thin. Twiggy's sixties figure is today about as fashionable as her eyelashes. Being thin leads to osteoporosis and, even worse, makes your head look too big. From a distance you look like a stick figure with a big pumpkin on top.

But being fat is no day at the beach, either.

Here's the plain truth via the AMA: "If you want to lose weight, you either have to consume fewer calories or exercise more, or preferably do both." There is no other way. Okay, so here's our guide.

CALORIES STILL COUNT

Chew on this for a while: One pound of fat equals 3,500 calories. You will gain a pound whenever you store 3,500 calories *more* than your body needs to maintain a certain weight. Therefore, if you are ten pounds overweight, it means you ate 35,000 more calories than you needed. We know you didn't mean to, really.

THE VERITAS ON VINO

Now let's talk a bit about alcohol. It tastes good, and you'd never know by the skinny Euros who drink wine like crazy that alcohol can make you hugely fat. Tragic but true. According to NBC's Dr. Art Ulene, here's what happens if you have just one measly drink a day: A daily beer will add fifteen pounds in a year, one "hard" drink each day adds seventeen pounds. Here's the really sad part: A glass of wine a day will add nine pounds to your body by the end of the year. Who ever said life was fair?

THE SALT OF THE EARTH

We all learned at birth about water retention. It is the cause of much misery and suffering, particularly around bathing suit season. Sodium (found mostly in salt) makes you retain water. You know this. We know this. Every woman knows this. Still, we eat salt like Lot's wife on a premenstrual rampage. An adult needs only 1.1 to 3 grams of the stuff a day, but the average American consumes 10 to 12 grams a day, thanks to processed and fast foods—*one half the toxic dose.*

THE SKINNY ON FAT

Your daily intake of fat should be only 20 percent, and no more than 10 percent of your fat intake should come from saturated fats. (Unsaturated fats tend to be solid at room temperature.) Good fat includes olive oil and all vegetable oils.

Learn how to read a food label. Food labels are written so that only an idiot savant can interpret them and so that you won't understand how much fat you're actually eating. Here's the poop: A gram of fat equals nine calories. Each gram of protein and each gram of carbohydrate contains four calories. You don't have to be Stephen Hawking to do the math. One makes you fatter than the other. Therefore it's important not only to calorie-count but also to read— and understand—the percentage of fat calories versus the total calories of any food.

If a single serving contains 100 calories, next check out the category "calories from fat." If it is more than 20–25 percent calories from fat, don't eat it. It's like swallowing cellulite. (Low-fat and fat-free food are still fattening if they have a lot of calories. Sorry.)

TAKE THE *S* FROM FAST FOOD

If you have any interest whatsoever in staying thin or even staying alive (which, depending on your current state of mind about your body, may in fact be one and the same), avoid anyplace that doesn't require you to get out of your car in order to order, get, or eat your food.

CARBS: THE HEM LENGTHS OF FOOD

Carbohydrates go in and out of fashion like hem lengths. One day everybody's carbo-loading; the next day carbs are out, and people treat you like you're Jeffrey Dahmer if you're caught eating pasta. At press time they were out.

Let's make life easier:

- Go the whole-grain route, whether it be bread, cereal, or pasta.
- Friendly carbs include starchy veggies (corn, peas, potatoes, yams, lentils, squash) and most fruits.
- Always go with three or more grams of fiber. Fiber fills you up.

PROTEIN

Every boomer babe knows about protein. We all suffered through the high-protein/low-carbohydrate diet days. Do you remember eating a pound of bacon with mayonnaise for breakfast? No wonder that crazy diet was popular. We now know it was a killer, but what a way to die(t). Get your protein from fish, turkey, chicken, egg substitutes, tofu, and beans, especially lentils.

SMALLER MEALS

As you get older, frequent smaller meals are digested more efficiently. Big meals at this stage end up being stored as fat, no matter how they went in.

WATER

If you don't drink lots of water, your body thinks it's in the middle of a drought, and you'll retain water like crazy. The more you drink, the more you'll flush your system and reduce water weight.

SIT DOWN

Eat slowly sitting down with your food on a plate, using napkins and utensils. Chew. Swallow. Keep the refrigerator door closed. Yes, it's still fattening if you eat standing up.

PORTION SIZE

A "serving" of meat or fish should be the size of a deck of cards, not a Frisbee.

DEPRIVATION DOS AND DON'TS

Dos: Steam, bake, broil foods. Use spices, mustard, lemon juice, and herbs instead of sauces, and pepper instead of salt.

Don'ts: Bag the butter, boot the sugar, and blow off the white bread.

A Babe's Guide to Torture
(aka Exercise)

Exercise. You can't live without it—unless you want to look like Mama Cass.

While it's generally not a good idea to be either obsessive, compulsive, or neurotically guilty, exercise is one area in life in which all three come in handy. You should be obsessive about setting up your exercise schedule and compulsive about sticking to it. If you miss a few days, you *must* feel a sickening sense of guilt. Then you need to visualize Kate Smith, the biggest thing on the small screen, singing "When the Moon Comes Over the Mountain"—only put your head on her body. Could Kate Smith have been a boomer babe? Could *anyone* whose bosom starts at the chin and ends at the knees? We don't think so.

When you get older, you lose muscle tone and the ability to metabolize food in any meaningful manner. Remember how matronly women in the fifties looked, long before they turned fifty? Men, too—Bing Crosby actually had a set of breasts. The next time the 1954 movie *White Christmas* is on TV, check out Der Bingel in his tank top. And he was a movie star!

No wonder baby boomers, haunted by images of the middle-aged folks of their youth, started the whole fitness boom of the eighties. Boomers have the burden of being the "youth generation," which gave them a desperate need to remain forever young (sexy), vigorous (sexy), attractive (sexy), and healthy (sexy). We started running, lifting, aerobics, and cross-training to suppress the fact that we couldn't stay twenty-five. While we might not look twenty-five, we sure don't look fifty either.

When we were growing up, the people who went to gyms were the Vic Tanney creeps, greasy musclemen on the back of comic books talking about physical culture and wearing funny-looking underpants. Still, the men's gyms were better than what went on in the ladies' "figure salons." Gym equipment for the "gals" was a nightmare in and of itself. Mostly it consisted of those jiggling belts that strapped around the hips, and the only change that occurred was permanent damage to internal organs. The Canadian Air Force came out with an exercise book in the late fifties that was considered revolutionary because it encouraged women to do push-ups! Of course, in the pictures, the women were working out in their uniforms.

Throughout this book, we keep talking about the advantages of exercise, and since you have no choice but to exercise, we'll give it to you one more time. First and most important, you'll look better. Second, you'll look better. Finally, you'll feel better. Exercise reduces the risk of so many old lady maladies: heart problems, weight gain, varicose veins, arthritis, high blood pressure, menopausal symptoms, osteoporosis, and Hadassah arms. You can eat more, too. Also, exercise combats Miss Grundy–like crankiness. That's because when you work out, your brain releases endorphins, those opiatelike substances that are about as close to high as you're going to get these days.

Exercise is as much a mental game as a physical one. Conquer the mental part, and the physical part will follow.

THE MENTAL GAME

Yogi Berra once said of baseball: "90 percent of this game is half mental." Remember this when you start to exercise. Stop decades of self-defeating litanies: "I'll never get in shape," "I don't have time," and "I didn't play sports as a kid." As the ads say, "Just do it," to which we add, "And get off your ass!"

Here are some tips to win the mental game:

DON'T START THE MIND F*#@%

This means telling yourself now is not the right time. This means coming up with excuses that range from the nurturing "Take it easy on yourself, you need rest more than anything else, you poor darling" to the abusive "You're a loathsome pig and nothing will ever get you in shape, I hate you." In between lies the big lie: "I'll do it tomorrow." Put your exercise bra on and shut your mind off.

FIGURE OUT HOW TO MAKE IT A HABIT

It sounds corny, but it works. It just has to be an essential part of your daily schedule. You should know yourself well enough by now to figure out what will get you off your keister. If what will get you to exercise is to make a workout date with a friend or join an expensive health club or sign up for aerobics classes or have a standing appointment with a trainer, then do it. Do whatever it takes.

BE PATIENT

You won't get results the next day or the next week. But it *will* pay off in time. Remember that crash exercise programs are about as smart, healthy, and effective as crash diets.

GET WITH THE PROGRAM, PART 1

Exercise is big business. There are as many different regimens and programs as there are episodes of *I Love Lucy*.

Find something that works for you and stick with it. If you
get bored with one program, try another.

CHECK YOUR EGO AT THE DOOR WHEN YOU HIT THE GYM

Gyms are filled with people who act like working out is a religion and they are the high priests. Ignore the stupid show-
offs who make really loud grunts and take themselves soooo
seriously. (With those dramatic facial expressions, you'd
think they were working on a cure for cancer instead of just
exercising.) Avoid anyone who asks you nosy questions like,
"How much do *you* lift?" These are generally the same people who will utter the most hostile words in the English lan-
guage: "Aren't you putting on weight?"

DON'T COMPARE YOURSELF TO ANYONE

Yes, there will be people at the gym who are built like Elle
MacPherson. Sure, there are some people out there with really great bodies. Don't look at them. You must realize that
they don't work, are really shallow, and, deep down, desperately unhappy.

DON'T GIVE UP

If you miss a few days, weeks, or even months, don't assume
you're a slug. Just try the Kate Smith visualization again and
get back on the program. We once read a discouraging stat:
It takes six months to start a good habit and just six weeks

to undo it. If you've gone past the six-week mark, just get back on the proverbial horse. Don't start the mind f*#@% that tells you it's all over.

MAKE A COMMITMENT

Make it to yourself, by yourself, and for yourself. "If your clothes don't fit, you must commit." Get religion, too. Tell yourself that by not going to the gym you are committing a sin, a sin of omission.

START OFF WITH A TRAINER

He or she will personalize a program and teach you proper form—the wrong form does you no good at all—and discipline. The steady appointment provides accountability: Think of a trainer as your superego. It's expensive, but if you can swing it, even just for a few months, you should do it. A good trainer will push you harder than you will push yourself and show you how to raise expectations for yourself.

A bad trainer will be cheaper and not as effective, but since, at this point, admittedly, you don't know your ass from an eggplant, the cheap trainer will still be great for you.

GET A PARTNER

Exercise, especially aerobic exercise, is easier and can almost be fun if you have a partner. But the big advantage is that it is highly unlikely you will *both* want to blow it off on the same day.

MAKE FRIENDS AND INFLUENCE PEOPLE

If you want a social life along with your workout, join a health club with a juice bar, Jacuzzi, pool, and lounge. (Linda and Rosemary, however, would have their fingernails torn out before they ever attended the Sunday brunch at their gym. Believe us, you have no idea. Every freeloader within twenty blocks can smell the free bagels and they eat like they've got four behinds—which, after brunch, they do.)

THE PHYSICAL GAME

GET A PHYSICAL

You're probably due for one anyhow since you are now—sorry—at an age where the old machine needs a checkup. You have new things to think about these days. Things like your heart, blood pressure, bone density, and even—hold on—your hearing! (Growing up listening to rock can be hell on the ears.)

EXERCISE THREE TO FOUR TIMES A WEEK

Sorry, but once a week doesn't make it.

JOIN A GYM

The main concern? Make it one close to where you work or live. Period. Second? Don't join one that will require you to wear a weight belt just to carry in the membership fee. In other words, unless you're loaded and don't care about spending big, you don't need to spend big. Most gyms have the basic equipment you need.

If you have a choice, join one that is *not* filled with young hard-bodies. What do they know about life anyhow?

Don't join one where there are yentas in full hair and makeup and hugely expensive workout wear. They'll only make you think you're working harder than you actually are.

Stay away from gyms that are overcrowded or smelly or have disgusting locker rooms, since that will only give the excuse you so desperately want not to go.

Many of the big chains have reciprocal agreements with other gyms around the country, so you can work out wherever you are. Or, for $10 or so, you can walk into any gym and work out for the day.

TAKE EXERCISE CLASSES

They can be fun. Okay, we lied, they're not really fun, but the group experience works for a lot of people.

DO IT AT HOME

If you are really self-disciplined, you can work out at home. Get some free weights, leg weights, a mat, and if you're rich, get a stationary bike, ski machine, or treadmill. If you'd rather kill yourself than buy exercise equipment, find a sturdy chair, a mop handle, rope, a towel, cheap free weights, and a used jump rope. Improvise.

What you need more than anything is a good exercise video- or audiotape. There are lots to choose from, although, happily, you can still turn your nose up at Debbie Reynolds videos. The general opinion is that the Jane Fonda Workout tapes are the best overall. (But, really, can we ever forgive Jane her new breasts and unseemly, un-PC behavior— swiping at the air with tomahawk chops during Atlanta Brave games?)

GET EQUIPPED

Get a good bra—think of it as your answer to the jockstrap. Get athletic shoes designed for the type of exercise you're doing. Get simple exercise clothes. That means leave your jewelry, makeup, perfume, leg warmers, and anything pink at home.

LISTEN TO MUSIC

It helps most people to listen to music. Aerobic classes were the best things to happen to disco since the Village People. Hard rock, disco, hip-hop, Latin are all great to get you pumped. Listening to Art Garfunkel drone "Bridge Over Trouble Waters" during your workout will hardly get your heart rate up.

WARM UP BEFORE

You must warm up for at least five minutes to get your pulse going and get the blood flowing into your muscles. Use the stationary bike. Run in place if you don't care what you look like.

Stretch before you get started. Use yoga stretches because they are great and graceful looking.

GET WITH THE PROGRAM, PART 2

Get someone who works at your gym to design an exercise program for you. But make sure he or she is a professional trainer and not someone who was selling scented candles the week before last. Failing that, a friend who's in great shape, has been working out for years, and doesn't hate you can help.

WALK THE WALK

Act as if you're a long-time jock. *Attitude is everything.*

TALK THE TALK

Here's a guide to gymspeak.

Abs: Stomach muscles

Bench press: Lifting weights while lying on a bench. Duh.

Bis: Muscles on the front of upper arm

Burn: It hurts.

Delts: Muscles of the shoulder

Gluts: Butt

Lats: Muscles of the upper back

Obliques: The part of your body formerly known as your waist

Pects: Chest

Pump: Exercise with weights

Quads: Front of thigh muscles

Reps: Repetitions

Roids: Steroids or hemorrhoids, whatever is applicable

Set: Repeating a specific number of reps of a specific exercise, as in three sets of ten reps each

SuperSet: Moving quickly back and forth between two exercises, kicking people off machines, if necessary

Traps: Muscles from shoulder to neck

Tris: Back of upper arm (the part that flaps)

Work in: Somebody wants to use a piece of equipment that you got to first and instead of knocking you off, he (it's usually a guy) says, "Can I work in with you?"

DRINK PLENTY OF WATER WHILE YOU EXERCISE

THINGS TO AVOID

- When lifting, avoid quick movements and don't use weights that are too heavy. On the other extreme, graduate from the three pounders.
- Don't rush through your program. Getting it over with faster doesn't work.

- If you are working with a trainer, make sure it's not one who admires himself or herself in the mirror all the time or one who calls you "lardass."
- Don't do jumping jacks. True, they are a great warm-up, but why should you relive high school humiliation? And if you looked like a jerk doing jumping jacks at fifteen, think of what you look like at fifty.

REST

Rest about one minute between sets and take one day of rest during the week. Like God.

DON'T HOLD YOUR BREATH

Learn the right way to breathe when you exercise. Inhale when you ease up and exhale on exertion.

LISTEN TO YOUR BODY

Know if you need to stop. Nothing cramps your exercise program more than an injury. But if you do get an injury, well, congrats girlfriend! You're now in ranks of those with a sports-related injury.

DON'T WEIGHT-TRAIN THE SAME SET OF MUSCLES TWO DAYS IN A ROW

This really defeats the purpose. If you are obsessed—and we hope you are—try weight training upper body one day and lower body the next.

MAKE AEROBICS PART OF YOUR PROGRAM

There's an endless supply of aerobics to choose from, but whatever you choose: **You must do it for at least twenty minutes, four times a week.**

Here's a partial list: forty-five different kinds of aerobic classes, jumping rope (said to be the perfect form of aerobic exercise but, like jumping jacks, hell on your image), running, walking, hiking, swimming, skiing, biking, games (tennis, racquetball, etc.), stationary bikes, StairMaster (said to give you a big butt), treadmill, VersaClimber, rowing machine, and much more.

FIND YOUR "COMFORT LEVEL"

That's the point where you are doing aerobics for an extended period of time at your personal training level *without* your tongue hanging out of your mouth.

DO IT ON THE ROAD

Exercise outdoors whenever you can. You'll do it longer and feel better afterward. Try running, walking, speed walking (if you don't mind looking odd), hiking, and biking. Start off slowly and increase your speed and resistance as you go along.

A note on running: There are as many arguments against running as for it. It's a great way to take off weight and clear your head. However, the older you are, the more potential you have for joint injury. You will go down a dress size but up two shoe sizes. Yet it *is* free, you can do it anywhere, anytime.

LIVE IT

Walk instead of drive when possible, hoof it up the stairs instead of taking the elevator or escalator; throw a pair of sneakers in your bag and keep an extra pair at work. That way you're always ready to hit the road.

Whether you're in the supermarket, on a conference call, or shaving under your arms, pull in your abdomen. When talking on the phone, slowly raise your legs, hold them up for a few seconds, and then slowly lower them. This works thighs and abdomen and won't put a run in your panty hose.

LEARN YOGA

After only a few classes, you will know enough yoga to do it for the rest of your life. You'll learn some important stretches and increase your endurance and flexibility. Plus, yoga firms up the body and quiets down the mind. Think Raquel Welch.

COOL DOWN AFTER

Don't stop abruptly even though you're so happy it's over.

NOTES ON THE RESISTANCE

MACHINES

The jiggling belt days are over. Instead, boomer babes are working out (and working in) alongside the guys, using weight-training machines. There is a machine for every part of your body, even ones that you never thought of as a problem, such as forearms. When you're doing it right, you should feel the contraction of the muscle. When you're doing it wrong, you will feel absolutely nothing and think to yourself, "Hey, this is easy!"

Every machine, except the odd throwback to Charles Atlas days, indicates how much weight you're lifting and how you can add extra weight as you progress. Know how much weight you're lifting. Then increase the amount.

A tip: Don't worry about building big muscles. It won't happen unless you're on steroids or are taking testosterone injections.

FREE WEIGHTS

No lesser a personage than Arnold Schwarzenegger prefers free weights to machines since they demand more of your body. They are great for isolating certain muscles and spot-training problem areas.

A tip: Please, please, please make sure your grip on the weight is firm. If for some reason you want to change your grip in the middle of a set, it's really smart to set down the weight and then start over. You don't want to put all this work into your body only to smash your face in.

THE BELLY OF THE BEAST

As much as you'd like to, don't forget about abs. Abs are a problem for most women, and the reason has to do more with evolution than eclairs. Most of us have an extra layer of fat built into our lower abdomens to protect our reproductive organs since nature has entrusted us with carrying on the species. And you have this fat whether you want to carry on the species or not. As with most things, this problem gets more acute the older we get, especially if you do love eclairs, so give abs special attention.

Cardinal rule of ab work: Keep your stomach muscles pulled in or else you'll get exactly what you're working so hard to prevent—a gut that sticks out. Granted, your protruding gut will be hard, not flabby, but unless you invite people to poke their fingers in your stomach, no one will know.

A tip: Sure, the commercials are annoying, but we recommend the Ab Roller. Since it helps isolate ab muscles, it does a lot of the mental concentration for you. Use it at the gym, and if you have room (and extra money), get one for the home as well. Sit-ups and the crunches that are currently in vogue really do the trick if you do them. Also, interestingly, it's okay to grunt during crunches but *only* during crunches.

Be realistic in your expectations for yourself. You'll never have the body Brigitte Bardot had in *And God Created Woman.* But no one else in the history of the world ever will either. And although BB was definitely a babe, she would never have made it as a boomer babe. On her fiftieth birthday, she took a long walk on a short beach after downing 100 Seconals. The only possible explanation for this behavior is that there must not have been any gyms in Saint-Tropez at the time.

sixteen

Lotions, Potions, and Notions to Make You Younger, Hipper, Healthier, and Thinner

Okay, we don't really know how to keep you from aging. Nor do we know how to keep your skin from wrinkling, keep your hips from saddle-bagging if you eat like a cow, or keep laugh lines from turning into crow's-feet. But we do have some very good suggestions that can keep you looking and feeling better than you should, considering how you abused yourself (admit it, now!) with drugs, sex, and rock and roll through the sixties and seventies.

But first you must forget that we grew up with the belief that people who went to health food stores and took loads of vitamins to prevent and cure illnesses were at best kooks and at worst Communists who vacationed at nudist colonies.

Here, then, a miniprimer on how to help everything from fatness to memory loss with vitamins, herbs, and healthy concoctions you can make from ingredients you'll find right in your own cupboard. (All right, you'll really find them there only if you happen to live in a health food store or if you're a midwife or something.)

APPLE CIDER VINEGAR

Claims: Weight loss, alertness, better joints, and more.

Have we got three words for you: apple cider vinegar!

According to Vermont folk medicine lore, drinking two teaspoons of apple cider vinegar (organic preferred) diluted in a glass of water first thing in the morning is a miracle fat cutter. It supposedly speeds up the metabolism, aids in digestion, and generally makes you thinner, healthier, and an overall better person. In fact, in the first week of drinking the incredibly vile potion each morning, Linda lost five pounds even though she ate pizza one night for dinner. Okay, two nights. And it makes you lose so much water weight in the first couple of days that you'll think you're on high-speed diuretics.

According to John Lust (we swear that's the guy's name!) in a book he wrote just about vinegar, titled, appropriately enough, *Cider Vinegar*, this remedy goes way, way back.

The only thing you really must remember is to brush your teeth immediately after drinking what Lust has the gall to call this "beverage." ACV is very tough on tooth enamel. You really don't need to be reminded of this, though, because it tastes so awful you'll be running to brush your teeth.

In addition to helping in weight loss, this magic potion also helps to: speed up healing, cure sore throats, restore mental alertness, improve that bad taste in your mouth in the morning, eliminate belching, make your nails stronger, improve calcium metabolism, eliminate eye twitching, stop joint creaking (by adding sodium chloride to the body), ease menstruation, improve blood clotting, improve hearing, and improve bladder efficiency so you're not running to the bathroom every three and a half minutes. Insomnia? Mix 2 teaspoons of apple cider vinegar with 2 teaspoons of honey in a glass of water at bedtime, to help you catch some zzzz's.

Who knew you could get thin, fall asleep, become a mental giant, grow your nails, *and* stop twitching all for $1.59? A bargain at twice the price!

Our personal conclusion: It can't hurt—and losing five pounds is probably as good as getting rich, finding the perfect man, and maybe even finding God. On the downside: You will wake up miserable each morning when you realize that you haven't died in your sleep and you will have to get up and drink the drink again.

ANTIOXIDANTS

Claim: Foe of free radicals.

Quick: What are free radicals? If you guessed Abby Hoffman, you're wrong, and if you guessed unstable molecules that contribute to aging, heart disease, and cancer, you're right!

Antioxidants are actually a group of vitamins that when taken together will stymie free radicals. In other words, they're good.

They are: vitamin E (400–1,000 IU), vitamin D (400 IU), vitamins B_5 and B_6 (400 mg), vitamin C (500–2,000 mg). Along with the vitamins, take the following minerals: magnesium, zinc, selenium, and beta-carotene.

GINKGO BILOBA

Claims: Memory restorer, circulation booster, hearing enhancer, headache helper, eye disorder improver.

If you are beginning to feel terrorized every time you happen to see someone you've known forever coming your way because suddenly you can't remember his or her name, take heart. Just in time for our midlife crisis comes a discovery of one of the oldest remedies on earth: ginkgo biloba.

The ginkgo biloba tree is about 280 million years old, give or take a few months. And it's probably been used for medicinal purposes for about that long.

So it's ironic that ginkgo biloba is now being proclaimed as the wonder plant. For one thing, clinical studies in this country and in Europe from the 1970s to the present day show astounding improvements in people suffering from Alzheimer's, basic memory problems, and other signs of aging when given 120 mg of ginkgo biloba extract every day for several months.

Americans come harder to nonprescription remedies than do Europeans and Asians. As a population we look askance at anything that even remotely smacks of holistic, natural, or homeopathic remedies. It took the Asians and Euros about fourteen minutes to jump on the GBE bandwagon. In fact, they are so convinced by the findings that they buy $500 million worth of the stuff every year. And not just extracts, but medicinal products as well, which have not yet been approved here by the FDA.

Meantime, Euros and Asians live longer and leaner than Americans, and they eat like crazy. Who's sorry now?

According to one booklet on the subject, *Ginkgo Biloba*, by Frank Murray, "Few herbal remedies have been as extensively researched as has ginkgo biloba extract, and the supplement seems to be one of the most useful therapies for many complaints."

The first day we took it, we had a giant memory surge that then leveled off to a slow rebuild. It was pretty remarkable—though totally useless—to be able to remember what movies Glenn Ford starred in. Of course, it would be better if we could permanently remember things like our own daughters' names, but at press time we were only a few weeks into the treatment.

If you are leery of trying GBE yourself, give it to the man in your life. It's also supposed practically to cure impotence, provided it's not caused by some horrid disease or, worse, his total disinterest in *you*. If his impotence is caused by his total disinterest in you, cure it by throwing the bum out.

We've been told that the ginkgo manufactured in Germany is the best, but we can't say for sure. What we can say for sure is that you should read up on the stuff and make a decision for yourself.

Our personal conclusion: Great rush in the first week, definite memory boost. Now, if we could only remember to take it. . . .

MELATONIN

Claims: Antiager, sleep inducer, stress reducer, anticancer agent, mood leveler.

If you go with the promoters, there is basically nothing that melatonin can't do. If you go with the detractors, there's nothing melatonin really does. Melatonin production does decrease naturally with age, so the obvious conclusion is that if you take melatonin orally, it will replace the hormone, which in turn will keep you young.

None of the experts agree on anything, though. What everyone does agree on, however, is that it definitely helps you fall asleep. And when you've got a great, natural night's sleep, you automatically look younger.

What we also know is that you need to take only minuscule amounts—less than half the 3-mg dose the pills are usually made in. Minuscule amounts give you the same benefits as the larger doses without the side effects, which can include a mild sleep hangover.

Our personal conclusion: We like it for a restful night's sleep. The jury's still out on the rest of it.

DHEA

Claims: Antiager; weight loser; heart helper; Alzheimer's alleviator; possible preventor of some cancers, AIDS, lupus; sex drive enhancer.

DHEA is, to say the least, controversial.

Since DHEA is produced by young (i.e., highly sexual) people, it is assumed that it will help you *stay* young (i.e., highly sexual). In fact, in 1996, claims that DHEA could enhance male sexual performance sent sales soaring. Either the men were too busy having sex to report in, or it didn't take, because according to *Time,* no evidence exists that DHEA affects your sex life one way or the other.

We did find one study that showed that women treated with DHEA had drops in cholesterol levels and boosts in energy levels and muscle and bone development.

What about weight loss and DHEA? Yeah, well, do we look any thinner to you?

Our personal conclusion: Probably a big nothing.

Hair Raising: The Babe's Complete Guide to Hair

There is one universal truth that's truer than any other universal truth: If your hair looks good, you feel good. Sure, that's a shallow way to think. So what?

A good haircut is the best nonsurgical way to alter your looks and lift your mood. A good haircut can make you look thinner, younger, hipper, and even happier. A bad haircut, or even the wrong haircut, can make you look older and—worse—fatter!

But even if you do find the perfect cut, by the time you get around to being fifty, sometimes your hair develops a mind of its own. There are plenty of reasons for that. For one thing, as your hair turns gray, the texture changes. For another, we've all been coloring, moussing, perming, straightening, blow-drying, and you name it for so long that the fact that we have hair at all is pretty remarkable.

Here then, advice from Damien Miano and Louis Viel of Miano-Viel Salon and Spa in New York City, who are credited with saving Linda's sanity—and hair—when a genius from Vidal Sassoon cut her bangs so short she looked like she'd gotten her head caught in a paper shredder.

HAIR DOS AND DON'TS

- Do get thee to a hairdresser if you are suffering from yearbook hair. If your hair looks anything like your picture—or anyone's picture, actually—in any yearbook, you are in big trouble. Only a professional can step in to remedy this dangerous situation.

- It's nice if your husband or boyfriend likes your hairdo, but for the sake of all that's holy, don't let him pick a hairdo for you. Most men—unless they are hairdressers themselves—think of hair as a separate entity from the actual woman they are with. They like Pamela Anderson Lee's hair. This has nothing to do with you, no matter who you are, unless of course your given name at birth was Barbie.

- When you see someone with a great haircut, stop her and ask her who her stylist is. She will not think of you as a serial killer and will in fact be happy to tell you. After all, you are complimenting her.

- There is no longer a rule that your hair should be shorter as you get older. Not that you should look like Crystal Gayle, but don't cut it off and start teasing it unless you want to look like your own mother.

- Too long, too short, too blond, too black, too permed, spiked (in any way at all), teased, too sprayed all add years to your looks.

- Avoid wedding hair, even at your own wedding. Women of great style always look touchable. Think Hepburn (Audrey)—her hair style was eternally chic and gorgeous.

- Keep current but keep it modified. It's a great thing not to be stuck in a mold, but trendy hair belongs on trendy kids. Remember how embarrassing you thought it was to see all those middle-aged people in the sixties at the Academy Awards aping *our* hippie hair? Take a current style you admire and have your hairdresser give you a modified version of it. If you are even tempted to go radical, think how Barbra Streisand looked when she fell in love with Jon Peters—and frizzed her hair and wore see-through clothing. She thought she looked like a rock star but we thought she looked like Minnie Pearl.

- Go to big-city salons for consultations. Don't be intimidated, for God's sake. Just be honest with the receptionist. Tell her you've got a big birthday coming up (your honesty doesn't have to extend to admitting *which* big birthday is coming up), and even though you don't *look* that age, and you don't *feel* that age, your hair is a dead giveaway. Which stylist would she recommend for a consultation? You'll probably have to wait until the stylist is free, but then so is the consultation.

- If you are trying a new stylist without a precut consultation, make sure the stylist talks to you first before you change into a robe, to see how you're dressed. It will tell the stylist reams about who you are and what you are comfortable with.

- Get several consultations and see if there is a common thread running through them all. If there is, it probably means it's something you should consider.

- Don't preprogram your stylist: Ask her what *she* thinks would look good on you. Then tell her what *you'd* like and then find a good common ground. Give a new stylist two tries to get it right. If you're miserable with a cut on the first try, give it a week.

- Every woman over fifty should have *some* bangs—it makes you look younger by making your face look softer rather than longer. (Faces elongate at puberty, which is why people with smaller features and less distance between the eyes and mouth look younger. Bangs fake this look.)

- Avoid shape on shape. If you have a square face, avoid a square haircut.

Avoid every variation of the following to avoid adding years to your age: wedge cuts, Charlie's Angel's layers, perms, streaks, anchor lady dos, big hair of any sort whether it's high or wide, stiff hair, ponytails with teased bangs (Connie Stevens), hair that's long in the back and short on the top (Connie, again), short teased layers, long teased layers, overprocessed hair, bad relaxers, hair that's too long and badly permed, dull hair, dull color. Please.

HAIR TO DYE FOR

- Gray hair always makes you look older. Period. Besides, it's very draining to the skin.
- If you look good with gray hair, you'll look spectacular as a blonde.
- Stay away from color extremes—no black, no platinum, and no superbright, artificial reds, unless you want to look like the mother on *Who's the Boss?*
- When picking a hair color, try to find the color closest to the shade you had as a teenager. Believe it or not, that's probably what will look best on you at this age.

- The rule about going lighter as you get older is old hat.

- Your skin color and eye color don't change, so why should your hair color? Most dark brunettes don't make great blondes. The operative word is softer, not lighter.

- Never color your hair in a single shade. Natural hair is many shades of the same tone, and a colorist achieves this by applying several shades to a base tone.

- Avoid hair color that is in tremendous contrast to your skin tone. You can end up with the Mary Mc-Fadden Kabuki look.

- If the color you dyed to get has no relation to any color that was ever created on any human head, it will look fake, and this will make you look older. There are no exceptions to this rule, by the way.

- There are very few human chameleons who can change their hair color every two minutes. Madonna is one; Annie Lennox and Linda Evangelista are others. Chances are good that you aren't any of them, so chances are good that changing your hair color like you change your clothes is probably not a great idea.

- Hair color is your most important fashion accessory. Be prepared to spend more time and money on it than you did when you were surfing and the streaks came naturally.

- When you see a colorist, you'll do better to bring an old picture of yourself than a new one of Claudia Schiffer. Frosting belongs on cakes, not on heads. Ash blond is not a good hair color—for anyone, actually. It's draining, and it's really the ultimate gray color with a fancy name. Avoid it.

- Above all else, keep the color warm. It will allow you to use less makeup and make you look younger and more approachable.

Making Up to Make It Big: The Babe's Complete Guide to Makeup

Nothing, repeat nothing, ages you quicker than outdated makeup and/or no makeup at all. Both make you look like you're kind of out of it, and that's the last place a real babe likes to hang out. According to Gary Greco, a New York City makeup artist, "Keeping who you are is very important— but so is updating yourself, by modernizing the look you're most comfortable with."

TIP-TOP TIPS

- Update your look! This might be terrifying for you, so Greco says to do your research and find out what makeup artists work in your area. It's always a good bet to go to the nearest big-city salon, which for sure will either have a makeup artist on staff or know where you can find a good one. A makeover lesson will generally run you from $60 to $100. You deserve it.

- What we all hate to admit is that at this stage of the game gravity is having its way with us. So reshape your brows to open up your face. Make the arch higher—it helps the brows look less droopy by giving you more space between the brows and the eye socket.

- Before applying mascara, wipe the wand with a tissue to avoid clumping. If you fail to do this, and are mistaken for Tammy Faye Bakker, don't say you weren't warned.

- To keep your mascara from drying out, twist the wand out of the tube—don't pump it up and down.

- The good news is that the makeup you spent hours learning to apply in the sixties is back, sort of. In other words, you don't need to stop using eyeliner, just modify, modify, modify. Go from black to black/brown or, better yet, dark brown.

- If you apply mascara without first curling the lashes, your eyes will look closed up instead of opened up.
- Learn to love color corrector. This is not concealer. It's stuff that counteracts the circles under your eyes according to your skin tone and is applied before concealer. Here's a skin tone/concealer color chart:

  Asian: Pink

  Mediterranean: Yellow

  African: Yellow or amber

  Scandinavian: Whitish
- Use a concealer that is *almost* the same color as your foundation.
- Liquid foundation looks better during the day, and cream during the evening.
- Choose your foundation by trying it on your neck. If you can't see it, it's the right shade for you.
- If you want to use eye shadow, don't even think about using the same color shadow as your eye color. For one thing, the color competes with your eyes for attention. For another, you will look like your Aunt Sadie if you use blue or green eye shadow.
- Lash conditioner is king. It gives you movie star lashes when you apply mascara on top.
- Your blush should match the color your cheeks turn after aerobics or, better, the color you turn when you *blush.* Nobody blushes in mauve or tan.

- For lipstick that sticks, cover your lips with concealer. Then outline them with a lip pencil. With the same pencil, draw vertical lines on both the top and bottom lips inside the outline. Fill in with lipstick in a matching or close-to-matching shade and rub lips together.
- Keep a little spray bottle filled with mineral water on your desk, in your car, in your bag, and spritz your face throughout the day. Dry skin lacks water, not only oil.

BABY-SOFT BODY

It takes twenty minutes for the body to absorb maximum moisture. Therefore, if your body skin is extra dry, as it can be in dry climates, or in air conditioning or heating, soak in a warm tub for twenty minutes, *then* add bath oil. (Alpha Keri is a good one because it sits on top of the water rather than dispersing in it.)

As you rise from the tub, the oil will adhere to your skin and lock in the moisture that's been absorbed by the bath. Or spray all over with Neutrogena Dry Oil when you step out of the tub. It's great because it goes on dryish, and since it squirts, you can reach your back.

Cosmetic Surgery: Is There Such a Thing as a Knee Job?

How it happens is no secret. *That* it happens has never been known to bring any joy whatsoever in civilized societies: looking older.

Somehow or other, you wake up one day and notice that the things that were attached to you the last time you looked are starting to detach. Is that a knee over your knee? And forget the old "Can you go braless?" test, wherein you placed a pencil under the breast fold crease, and if the pencil fell straight to the ground, your breasts were perky enough to go braless.

The last time you tried that test, though, you were able to hold up a laptop under the left breast alone. Hey, it happens. Who knows, if you didn't give birth to those rotten kids, you might still have breasts like Pamela Anderson Lee. Why? Because you, like her, would have lots of money socked away by now and could afford new breasts.

Getting older is one thing, but looking older is a real pain in the ass. One day people are shocked that you are old enough to have a ten-year-old child and the next they aren't in the least surprised that you have a twenty-two-year-old who's graduating from college. Well, take heart, girl. There *is* help. It ain't cheap, but then neither are you!

So how did you (we/us) start looking your (our) age? Simple. The aging process is more than just an accumulation of years. For one thing, how you age is encoded in your genes, one more thing you can blame on your parents. Add to that life and living factors, and you've got the makings of aging.

Sure, if you never went into the direct sun, smoked, drank, pursed your lips, flew on a plane, yawned, leaned on your palm, or smiled, and if you ate only nutritious, non-fattening foods so that you always maintained a perfect weight and didn't need to diet, and had a great gene pool, chances are better than good that you'd still have the skin of a twenty-year-old. But you'd probably be dead of boredom.

Don't misunderstand. None of these things—leaning, yawning, smiling, smoking, drinking, or eating crapola—in and of itself causes your skin to go to the dogs, but all of these things together contribute to and accelerate the aging process.

But come on! Even the boy in the bubble laughed and ate junk food from time to time. If you never did anything, or went anywhere, you'd be wrinkle free all right, but you'd also be a big nun.

And there's one more thing, and it's a big one: When we were teenagers, we all tanned and sunned ourselves until we burned and peeled. *And* we slathered baby oil on at the beach—the equivalent of frying skin. Sun causes wrinkles. Check out your backside. The reason it doesn't have the lines on it that your face has is that you don't regularly expose your backside to the sun, and you don't do all the other things with it that you do with your face, like smoke. At least we hope not.

Also, it takes around fifteen to twenty years for sun damage to show on the skin. So the damage you did to yourself way back when is showing up now as lines, wrinkles, and—yes—age spots. For our purposes, however, let's call them sun spots. It's just easier.

Gerald Imber, M.D., a plastic surgeon, recently wrote a book called *The Youth Corridor*, in which he says the skin is only (are you ready?) fifteen to one twenty thousandths of an inch thick. Even so, it keeps everything covered up pretty well and is the first line of defense against the elements. Unfortunately, it's also the place that shows the effects of stress, environment, acne, and you name it first.

FACING UP

The first signs of aging on your face show up as smile lines outside the eyes, followed by lines under the eyes. Next, the cheeks get wrinkly, and the skin gets drier. (Quit now, if you can't hear any more.) Discoloration on the face and little lines at the corners of the mouth and then above the lip can next start to show up. Suddenly, the jaw looks fuller, and small fatty pouches show up alongside the mouth. Help! Let's throw ourselves into the river!

Okay. You haven't done that? Let's see what we can do about slowing time down a little. Let's start first with fine lines, wrinkles, and discolorations. As we (the pig in the python again) age, we take the swell of the population with us. Therefore, every day new and marvelous treatments both topical and surgical that can turn back the clock are being introduced. Like we said earlier, we ain't going down without a fight, and the medical industry, if not the cosmetics industry, is hip to our needs.

Let's start with the topical stuff.

SUNBLOCK

First, let's talk about preventing wrinkles, or at least preventing more wrinkles. According to Dr. Peter Linden, a plastic surgeon with offices in New York City, Nantucket, and London, "Sunblock is the most inexpensive, noninvasive preventive medicine we have. Still, people just don't bother—they *still* like to tan, despite everything we now know." The equation is: Tan = wrinkles = misery.

Get three or four different brands of baby sunblock and keep switching so that you don't develop an immunity or sensitivity to any one brand.

Use it on your face and hands every day, even when you aren't sunbathing, swimming, or spending much time out-of-doors. You won't regret it. Trust us.

EXFOLIANTS

Moderately priced scrub cleaners with grainy texture. Exfoliant scrubs (they range from the low-end $1.99 drugstore apricot pit variety to the high-end $100 department store crushed pearl variety) should be a twice weekly ritual. A good moisturizing exfoliant takes off the topmost dead layer of skin cells and leaves your skin looking refreshed and healthy.

After exfoliating, your skin should look like you've been out for a good run or, better yet, just finished having incredible sex!

ALPHA HYDROXY (AKA FRUIT ACIDS)

Creams and lotions that act as a mild skin peel and collagen booster. Alpha hydroxy potions come at every price point from the drugstore variety at a few dollars to the department store cosmetics counter varieties that will set you back anywhere from $30 to over $100. The over-the-counter kind will not reach higher concentrations of 10 percent, which shouldn't cause more discomfort than a mild irritation.

The kind a cosmetic surgeon or dermatologist will use on you can go as high as 70 percent concentrations. Those are obviously much more effective and in some cases can cause real irritation. The treatments are done over a series of weeks. The result is overall clearer, less-wrinkled skin. The fees range from $100 to $300 per session, depending on the geographic location and the doctor's rep.

RETIN-A

This was a prescription item for acne. It worked very well. What also happened to the acne sufferers was a surprisingly overall clearing of the skin, the disappearance in some cases of precancerous lesions, and—yes—in adult-onset acne, wrinkles started disappearing. Make no mistake. It's very drying. It's also very harsh and, luckily, new formulations are making it less irritating. You start with 0.25 and work up to stronger strengths over several months. To keep the action going, you have to keep using the medication.

You must get a prescription for Retin-A from a doctor, so it gets kind of pricey once you add on the doctor's visit fee, but it's worth it.

Yes. It does clean up your skin and encourages the collagen to act as it did when you were younger.

PLASTIC SURGEON TIME

If you've tried the rest and now are ready for the big time, you're going to need to see a plastic surgeon, or at the least a great dermatologist for the following treatments. We haven't included everything, because this isn't a medical book, and anyway, who besides Cher and Michael Jackson can afford all this stuff?

And the reality is that once you start, you can become addicted and have a habit worse than heroin. And even more expensive.

More important, look at what happens once you become addicted. Michael Jackson looks like a nightmare Kabuki dancer and Cher looks like she hasn't closed her mouth in five years and would melt in the sun. So before you start, know what you're getting yourself into.

Michael Sachs, M.D., a New York plastic surgeon, supplied us with a lot of these facts. We trust him because we've seen his work *and* worked with him on stories at both *New Woman* and *Cosmo.*

Here's the best of what's available and how much it costs.

COLLAGEN

Cost: $300–$500 per dose.

Duration: A few months.

This is the substance that keeps your skin elastic. As you get older, you lose collagen and your skin starts to look older.

You can't apply collagen topically and expect it to do any-thing, because the molecules of collagen in creams are larger than human skin molecules and can't be absorbed. Collagen injections do, however, work, especially in the lines from the nose to the chin and the vertical ones on the forehead. The good news is that the injections fill in the lines. The bad news is that they last only a few months. More good news is that you can keep having collagen injections when the last one wears off up to two times a year or so.

Then there are the more involved treatments. Der-mabrasion, skin peels, and the newest—laser treatments. They all remove surface wrinkles, but they aren't all so great. If you walk around any big city, you'll see hordes of shiny ladies—the women who've been peeled, buffed, and lasered to the point that they have nearly transparent skin. Not great.

DERMABRASION

Cost: Anywhere from hundreds to thousands, depending on the area treated.

Not used so much anymore. This is a sanding wheel—picture a dental wheel that's rough. The doctor literally sands your face. The problem is that as the wheel goes around, cells stick to it, and some cells can get stuck back on the skin on the next pass. This causes those little whiteheads to form. The healing is not easy and the scabs are pretty thick.

LASERS

Cost: At least $1,000 per area treated.

The CO_2 laser seems to be the wrinkle remover of the moment. Remember seeing those horrifying pics in the tabloids of Dolly Parton right after laser? She looked like her skin had been burned off. It had.

The good thing we're told about lasers is that the computer controls the depth of the beam into the skin, so it's consistent and supposedly accurate. It's good on lines, especially the ones around the lips.

FAT INJECTIONS

Cost: $200–$800.

Duration: A few months or up to a year (yeah, sure).

Why someone would want to walk around looking like she was beaten up and ended up with a fat lip is beyond us. But look around. Everyone, it seems, is trying to look like Mick Jagger. In too many cases, though, great big puffy lips end up looking like the lipee was sucking on a tailpipe. Fat injections aren't, of course, only for the mouth. You can get fat injected into cheek folds and into sunken areas of the face. The always shameless Geraldo Rivera had the fat from his butt injected into his face. On the air. What some people will do for show biz.

It doesn't last more than a few months on anyone we've seen, but surgeons swear it can last up to a year.

THE WHOLE NINE YARDS: THE FACE-LIFT

Cost: $8,000–$20,000.

Duration: Your skin ages at the usual rate, but it's starting on a tighter canvas now. You may want another one in five to fifteen years.

Rule: You must let only a board-certified plastic surgeon perform surgery on you. Period.

Whether you admit it or not, you are secretly thinking about a face-lift. It can't be helped. It's encoded in our genes. You turn fifty, you begin to think like Zsa Zsa Gabor. You know it's happening when you find yourself pulling your cheeks up with your fingers every time you sit in front of the mirror to make up. We are programmed to do this, so there's no escaping the pull technique.

But if you really want to see what you'd look like with a face-lift, forget the pull technique. Dr. Peter Linden recommends this test: Lie on your back and hold a hand mirror in front of your face. If you like the way you look, you'll like the way you'd look with a (good) face-lift. "Good" in this case is not a relative term. There is one universal truth to all plastic surgery: If you can tell it's been done, it's not good. The goal shouldn't be to look twenty again, the goal should be to look the way we *want* fifty to look. In other words, like a boomer babe, but one with incredibly great bone structure. You want people to envy your incredible gene pool, not your doctor's talent.

And most important, you want to look very well rested, not like you've been laid to rest.

It's a three-to-four-hour procedure that improves sagging jowls, loose neck skin, and excess fat by tightening muscles. No matter what they tell you, you won't really know how you will look for about six months after the surgery. It takes that long for everything to fall nicely back into place.

EYELID SURGERY

Cost: About $4,000.

Duration: Your skin ages as it normally would. The difference is that you are now starting with tighter skin, so you'll look younger longer.

This surgery tightens and unpuffs the upper and lower lids. It can be great, or it can be awful. Burt Reynolds, for example, had it done, and now he looks like a Mongol. Aside from the possibility of blindness, difficulty closing the eyes, and the horror of getting a flat-out bad job by a bad surgeon, good eyelid surgery can stave off the AARP police for a few years.

THE BOOB JOB(S)

You can make them bigger. You can make them smaller.
Reduction

Cost: $6,000–V15,000.

Duration: Depends. If you gain weight, you can have huge breasts again.

If you want to have smaller breasts, know that you will be left with permanent scars and possibly end up with uneven nipples and a permanent loss of feeling. Of course, if you have massive breasts, you probably don't have much feeling in them anyway. It's tough surgery, but the women who've had it claim to be happier and freer than they have ever been before.

Enlargement

Cost: $6,000 and up.

Duration: Your breasts will stay up forever, but since they took the soft silicone implants off the market, you may end up with rock-hard basketballs sitting on your chest.

Not everyone wants to be Pamela Anderson Lee, although more fifty-year-old babes are taking it all off for *Playboy* than ever before. You should know that there is a possibility of infection and hardening scar tissue. The implant could rupture (unlikely), and there could be a reduction in feeling.

If, however, it's always been your dream to lie on your back and have your breasts sticking up like rockets bound for Jupiter, this is the procedure for you.

THE KNEE JOB

Sorry. We only tempted you with that title. There is no such thing. Get on the leg machine, make a novena, and hope that your knees don't fall somewhere around your ankles. Whoops! There they go!

twenty

We Should Have Been Reading *The Prince* Instead of Waiting for Him

Has it ever occurred to you that during the seventies, half of the population (male) read *The Prince*, while the other half (female) read *The Sensuous Woman*?

While we "girls" were demanding our right to work alongside men and reading how to please them in bed, the men were figuring how to get to the top and get on top, and how to do *everyone* in.

Boys were brought up to be successful, and girls were brought up to marry successfully. But in spite of our upbringing, our generation decided we wanted it all—

successful relationships and successful careers. We fought against the Donna Reed tradition and we won. Sort of. We made giant strides, but in many ways, we took on too many jobs.

We went to work and were grateful that we had a shot at real careers, not just jobs. However, we kept our night jobs too—cleaning, cooking, food shopping, raising the kids, doing homework with the children. Liberation was very exhausting. As the Italian journalist Oriana Fallaci once said, "What did liberation give us, really, but another job?"

Consider our history. In elementary school we wore dresses, making it easier for boys to see our underpants. We didn't really play sports (certainly not on after-school teams). And even though we were better students than the boys, our teachers had fewer expectations of us.

Then came the sixties. Even as revolutionaries, we accepted our place—behind the men who were behind the barricades. We never even questioned statements like Stokely Carmichael's famous, "The only position for a woman in the movement is prone."

We didn't beef, because we were still taking our baby steps. Remember, up until then, the only alternative to marriage for women was the dreaded Career Woman Syndrome (CWS).

To be a career woman meant a life of wearing your lipstick over the lip line, unsatisfying sex, hangovers, and worse—looking like Miss Hathaway in *The Beverly Hillbillies*. In short, you would be everything Donna Reed wasn't—

childless and drinking alone in a mannish suit without a shirtwaist to call your own.

Career women, by definition, did not have children. If they did, we all knew they would have to end up like Veda Pierce, daughter of Mildred Pierce. You remember Mildred Pierce, Joan Crawford's most famous (and fabulous) character, don't you? Veda not only slept with her stepfather, but then to further torture her mother, bumped off the son of a bitch when he wouldn't divorce Mildred for her.

What choice did Mildred have, really, but to take the rap for her kid? After all, she *was* a career woman! She "went to business." It was only right that her daughter would turn out to be a no-good tramp and murderer!

Despite it all, we boomer babes did go to business and even became CWs.

We are working harder—bringing home the (low-fat) bacon and cooking it too. We're making a difference politically. Don't forget that in 1996, it was *women* who reelected President Clinton. As a recent syndicated article by Steven Holmes pointed out, "The growling voice of the angry white man was drowned out by the softer tone of the soccer mom, and issues like family leave and day care were forced into the political debate." Women knew that here was one president who truly loves women. Okay, maybe too much . . .

Life sure has changed since we grew up in "honey, I'm home" households. America of the fifties and sixties idealized the nuclear family. God forbid a woman was a divorcee. We all knew that it meant that she was either abandoned or a fast woman—there was, we were taught, no other possibility. She had two options: find another husband—quick—or move back home with Mom and Dad.

Boomer babes changed all that. We legitimatize being single. But more important, we legitimatize single-parent families, making it a better option than staying in lousy marriages. Moms started becoming the breadwinners—not only because we wanted to but also because we had to. After all, necessity is the mother of empowerment.

We need to elect more women, support other women in the office, learn to trust other women, and, most important, help other women network the way men do. They read *The Prince*. They know what's what. We've reached higher than any generation before us—now we have to start helping other women get there too.

Remember, the biggest advantage to being this age is that we've seen it, done it, felt it, got it, missed it, and amazingly we haven't flipped out. Come close but that's about it.

At our age it's okay to compromise. It's not okay to plead and apologize for getting there.

NEW RULES

Okay	NOT Okay
Picking up the check	Getting stuck with the check
Supporting your husband and family	Not getting child support from your ex-husband

Okay	NOT Okay
Endless evaluations of the Super Bowl	Endless evaluations of you
Doing the housework	Doing all the housework yourself
Giving your kids an allowance	Getting an allowance yourself
Deodorant	Feminine hygiene spray
Handing over the remote control to your man	Giving your remote man control over you
Miserable in-laws	Miserable mates
Believing that shit happens	Believing that shit always happens to you
Flirting at work	Sexual harassment at work
Being passed over for a promotion	Being passed over for a man who's less qualified
Working like a man	Being paid like a girl

twenty-one

Grown Kids: You Can't Live with Them and You Can't Kill Them

Our generation has been called a lot of things, but as we get older, the terms get considerably less flattering. Now the "youth generation" is the "sandwich generation," meaning we are sandwiched between teenage children who don't want to know us and parents who forget they ever knew us in the first place. When it comes to your teen, have you noticed the strange phenomenon that takes place as he or she gets older? You somehow, miraculously, become less of an asshole. Then, just when your kids are getting adorable again, off they go to college.

What mother can be dry-eyed at the sight of her little birdie leaving the nest? (Answer: Any member of British aristocracy, since they all send their children to boarding school as soon as they start to walk or, of course, Joan Crawford.) But for us, it's a wrenching, poignant moment. After you've moped around for a few days or weeks, something happens. Slowly, softly, an inner voice emerges, saying, "Free, free, free at last." When you ask yourself the eternal question, "Should I kill myself or go bowling?" you answer with a resounding, "Yes, bowling, yes!"

Thus, boomer babes were born to dispel the myth of the empty nest syndrome.

(A brief aside: The baby boom generation never paid any attention to the traditional timing of life's markers, even when it came to marriage and children. So it's not surprising that while you are seeing your youngest off to college, the girl who borrowed your Cliff Notes of *The Scarlet Letter* is just ushering her first child to first grade. If you're the Cliff Notes borrower, move on. Ditto if you're Mia Farrow. Finally, if you've never had children, this chapter has about as much relevance to your life as a five-day passport to Disney World.)

The term "empty nest syndrome" is a throwback to Barbara Bush's generation when women lost their sense of identity as children grew up and left home. There was no one to care for but George or hubby, who never wanted to be home in the first place. They call it a syndrome, meaning it's a problem and you're supposed to feel crappy, use-

less, and tormented with the question, "Who am I now?"
There's no one to bake cookies for. Life is empty, so bring
on the Valium.

Women of today are so much younger—at the same age—
than women of previous generations. Our fifty is not Barbara Bush's fifty, and we will never be as old as she was at
forty. Sorry, Babs, but that's just where it's at.

We are the first generation of women who went to work
with ambition, whether we had a husband or not. We actually liked working. Good thing, too, because right now less
than 7 percent of American families are composed of a
breadwinner father and a stay-at-home mother. We dumped
the fifties cult of domesticity while raising liberated kids,
even if we did wind up doing most of the child rearing.

The only modern mothers who are truly devastated by
children leaving for college are the ones who went apoplec-
tic at soccer games, running the length of the field scream-
ing their kid's name. They didn't have a life back then, and
it's doubtful that they will have one now.

While it's true that mother-child love is the most precious
expression of love, it is also true that it's great to get the
bathroom back. It's bliss finally to have time for yourself
and to listen to your own brand of rock. You can eat in bed
and, of course, you don't have to make any meals unless
you, personally, feel like eating. Or unless you have a mate
who acts like he's one of your children.

Boomer babes, who never have played by the rules,
should look at the empty nest syndrome as a malady that af-

flicted previous generations defined by their motherhood. It's a myth as far as we're concerned, since when our children are launched from home, we know it's a sign of a job well done—unless they're in prison or have joined the Church of Scientology. Whether they've gone to college, jobs, ashrams, Hollywood, or marriages, they're off and becoming their own people. (And in case you haven't noticed, your children have been separating from you, emotionally, for the last couple of years anyhow.) Congratulate yourself and begin to reclaim your life.

This doesn't mean, of course, that you should start dancing around the house in your underwear, although you can if you want to. What it does mean is that you are your own person once again and not somebody's mother. Here are just a few of the ways your life can be renewed:

- You can be sexual once again, something you could never wholeheartedly be around your kids. If children were comfortable with their mother's sexuality, Hamlet would have never gone nuts and Veda Pierce wouldn't have become a killer. The house is empty, meaning that you can do what you used to do way back when you weren't supposed to do it—have sex! You can develop a better sex life with your own husband (if you still have one). Failing that (and it usually does), you can develop one without him.

- You can be spiritual once again. The baby-boom generation, more than any other in history, eschewed formalized religion while at the same time becoming more spiritual. Of course, smoking pot at the time helped us in our mystical quest. When the kids are gone, you can meditate to your heart's content without them making noises or making fun of you. You can return to the religion you were born into or you can be fashionable and become a Buddhist. Without having to yell about dirty socks or empty orange juice cartons in the refrigerator, you will be automatically elevated to a higher plane.

- You can take classes. No, we're not suggesting you do what Rodney Dangerfield did in *Back to School* and follow your children to their campus and sit in their classroom. Instead, since you don't have to wonder about their book reports or why they spit salsa on their algebra homework, you can broaden your own horizons. Take flying, Italian, or mambo lessons. Study the guitar, the balalaika, whatever the hell you feel like.

- You can focus on your career or develop a new one. Now that you're not pulled in fourteen different directions from gymnastics to projectile vomiting to softball to you-name-it, you can be one of those people you've seen at the office who don't need to race home to get supper and help with homework. You can get in early since you're not spending the morning bellowing over and over, "Get out of bed! Now! I'm not saying this again!" You, too, can be the glamorous businesswoman, dining with important clients in smart restaurants while tossing your head back and laughing.

- Order is back in your life. Now something that you left on your bureau on Monday morning is *still there* on Friday evening! With this comes mental order as well. You're more organized without even trying.

- Privacy is back. Also, a bonus: You can start or finish your day without being taunted with the cry, "Moommmm, you have a wedgie."

- You can reclaim the following, which for years were only an illusion: the phone, TV, VCR, Blockbuster card, stereo, your CDs, the shower, the only dry towels, anything good to eat in the refrigerator, toothpaste, and *People* magazine.

- You don't have to steal time for exercise. No more sneaking out for a facial. Go take a long bath or get a hedonistic massage. Finally, and this may sound heretical, you can go to a spa.

- You can gossip outrageously about anybody, anytime, and say anything without worrying that your kids will overhear and repeat it at times designed to cause you the greatest amount of discomfort.

- Your mornings *and* evenings are free. Your weekends are liberated with only minimal trips to the supermarket since milk and toilet paper last longer. You can sleep late, go to bed early, meet your boyfriend at a hot sheets motel, go to the movies on *weeknights*, wear a new negligee to bed and shock your poor husband, make whatever you feel like for dinner.

- You can hang out. This means you can see more of your friends—important always to boomer babes since we are the first generation to redefine notions of family. Modern society has displaced the nuclear family, so many of us learned to make our friends our family, relying on friendships rather than blood ties.

- You can be almost guilt-free. There are fewer times when you absolutely have to be someplace, get somebody, or do something.

- Your phone messages will no longer fall into the black hole of telephone messages, which always happens when kids answer the phone. They never feel the need to inform you of your phone message because, to them, your callers are invariably old, boring, and unimportant.

- You never, ever, have to go to Orlando, Florida, again.

- You never have to figure out how much to pay the sitter *or* take the sitter home.

- You can experience something you haven't experienced at home in many years: silence. When Rosemary was in her ninth month of pregnancy, back in 1977, she was lucky enough to take a

Lamaze class with the famous champion of natural childbirth, Elisabeth Bing. At the end of the class, Ms. Bing asked all the first-time expectant parents to be absolutely quiet, no coughing, shuffling, heavy breathing. Then she whispered softly, "Listen." After a few minutes, she explained, "That is the sound of absolute silence. Enjoy it. After next month you won't hear it at home again for many, many years." She was right.

Still, we miss them. We love them and we have to keep reminding ourselves that they haven't dropped off the face of the earth. They just grew up, and that's exactly what they're supposed to do.

IF YOU CAN'T GO HOME AGAIN, HOW COME THEY'RE HERE?

They're baaaaaack!

Just when you get used to the empty nest, you get hit with a full house again. A full house of grown children! All of a sudden, the belief in communal living that you were spouting in the sixties goes down the toilet in the nineties. Or it would, except the toilet is always backed up since the house is now so full.

Most of the times when children move back, whether it's after college or after having their own apartment for a while, the reason can usually be summed up in one word: financial.

That's actually good news, since it means that it's not because your apron strings are three miles long or they desperately need your cooking or are afraid to be alone in the dark.

It's just that in this new world that our children inherited, jobs (if they can get one) don't pay much and rents are a fortune. Many of them are burdened with hefty college loans. This is quite a contrast to how we started our careers in the early seventies. When we got our first jobs, the starting salary was peanuts but we could get a dumpy "starter" apartment for peanuts as well. Now starting salaries are still peanuts but starter dumps are outrageously expensive, if you can even find one.

As Allen Schnaiberg, professor at Northwestern University, observed: "Housing costs have risen dramatically. And white-collar employment is shrinking, even as the number of college graduates continues to rise each year. A diploma no longer offers you much hope of gaining access to the executive washroom, unless you are there to clean it." There's an irony here: Our kids grew up so much faster than we did—in an R-rated world seeing condom ads on TV—yet they are forced to return home in adulthood. We grew up with Doris Day staying a virgin, and the raciest print ad we saw featured a woman in a ball gown with the cryptic headline, "Modess, because." Yet we could afford to move out as soon as we got a job. Go figure.

The 1993 census reported that 58 percent of all children under twenty-five had returned home, a phenomenon that has been called boomeranging. After leaving the nest, the birdies are spreading their wings and heading . . . back home. For many of us parents, this is the last thing we want. But for others, it's even better having them around the second time.

Neale Godfrey, former president of the First Women's Bank, offers some advice on arranging peaceful coexistence with your grown children. She suggests that you have a written agreement between you and your adult child that lists issues that need to be addressed when your child becomes, in effect, your tenant: rent, utility costs, household chores, car, and food budget. Spell out the arrangement, which should be directly related to whether your child is employed or not. You may feel like Gypsy Rose Lee's mother who charged her daughters for meals or—do we need to say it one more time?—Joan Crawford. But don't. Those mothers were dealing with children, not grown-ups. And remember that financial responsibility is a gift, since at some time your kids will be off on their own. They will. We promise.

Of course, you can let your kids stay rent-free so they can save money and soon be off, but even then there still must be ground rules relating to their sex life (and yours). If your children aren't comfortable with your boyfriend or a significant stranger spending the night, they should arrange to sleep elsewhere when he does stay over. It's your house. If you're not comfortable with your children's boyfriends or girlfriends spending the night, they should arrange to sleep elsewhere. It's your house. There should be an understanding about their entertaining and your entertaining, and you shouldn't wait up for them any more than they should wait up for you. Once it is understood, there's less room for resentment on either side.

Rule: Respect each other's privacy. They're not teens anymore, so don't treat them that way—it's not good for them and even worse for you. They're grown-ups who might actually like shopping and cooking, so let them. Of course they haven't matured to the point where they will enjoy cleaning, but they are too old to be the slobs you brought up. Roommates who are not their mothers wouldn't stand for it, so you shouldn't either.

This is the way it's going to be for a while. All the parents we've spoken to are happy to have their kids back home. They're back and they're mature and they don't find you gross anymore. They are the greatest companions for you, since, let's just say it, they are *your* kids. You've been the biggest influence on their values, character, sense of humor, and personality. Therefore, what else can they be but the most wonderful, decent, smartest, funniest kids in the world? You gotta love 'em.

twenty-two

Aging Parents: If It's Not One
Thing, It's a Mother

We are, perhaps, the first generation of women who are totally unprepared to care for our aging relatives. It's not that we don't know how. After all, when we were growing up, it was still commonplace for Grampa or Aunt Ethel to come and live—and die—with us.

Why, then, are we so unprepared to do for our parents what our parents did for their parents? For one thing, the nuclear family, where the dad worked and the mom didn't, where there were lots of children, and extended families were the norm, is now as rare as talking dogs. It was easier way back then to fit another person into the household than it is now. In addition, our parents, unlike us, probably didn't have to deal with new spouses, horrifying stepchildren, and/or lovers in the house. In fact, unless you grew up in Appalachia or something, your parents definitely didn't have to conceal any of those things from Aunt Ethel.

Of course, in the fifties and sixties, there weren't all those machines that could unnaturally extend Aunt Ethel's life another twenty years after a stroke left her incapacitated. She generally died a natural death from pneumonia, bronchitis, the flu, whatever, after living a reasonable amount of time with your family. "Miracle" drugs did not keep Aunt Ethel alive, although she suffered from Alzheimer's well past the time she would have been happy to move on to that big BarcaLounger in the sky.

The great news is that our parents are around longer to be with us, and more important, to be with their grandchildren. And in case you haven't noticed, a grandparent's love may be the only true unconditional love in the universe. Unless your kids are the Menendez brothers.

The bad news is that at some point we will probably be faced with the nightmare of long-term care for elderly parents. We can't afford—financially or emotionally—to give up our careers to care for aging parents, aunts, or uncles. And who besides the Kennedys and Arnold Schwarzenegger (who are intermarried anyway) can afford the fifteen hundred to ten thousand dollars or so a month it will cost to feel miserable about sticking our parents into a nursing home where they will be miserable themselves? It makes you long for the good old days when a million people were crowded into your house and you had to share your bedroom. Sort of.

How could this happen to *us*—a generation of naked, pot-smoking, antiestablishment, hippie freaks?

All right, we're stuck with it. Now what do we do about it? A friend said the only good thing about his mother's Alzheimer's disease was that she forgot she hated him. Laughter helps in the face of reality.

Here, then, the reality. Jane Falkenstein, M.D., a baby boomer herself and a geriatric specialist at Beth Israel Medical Center in New York, tells us that studies show that if the husband (that would be your father) gets frail first, the wife (that would be your mother) will do everything in her power to care for him until the bitter end. That's good for you.

However, statistics show that if the mother gets frail first, the father hasn't a clue how to cope. Caregiving is not something that our father's generation of men is prepared for. They cannot deal with seeing—let alone caring for—a totally incapacitated wife. Why does this come as a shock to you?

And, horribly, it's often the same with sons (that would be your brother, by the way).

So the burden may in fact fall solidly and completely in your lap. This as you may have guessed won't exactly add to your allure as a babe. Your first and of course best option is to keep your folks at home—their home—as long as possible. You can keep the best track of them that way, and there is usually excellent at-home care available everywhere. But it's pricey. Unless, of course, your parents are indigent, in which case they are entitled to Medicaid, which means you are home free (pun intended). Medicaid basically pays for all kinds of at-home care, but only when there is a documented medical need. As long as your parents' doctors and the hospital social workers think that at-home care is required and more cost-efficient than keeping them in the hospital (which it always is) or in a nursing home (which it may or may not be), they'll get it.

You must understand that the government's main function is to punish as many hardworking people when they are most vulnerable as possible. Therefore, retirement to the feds is the total realization of the no good deed goes unpunished principle. If your parents, for example, carefully sequestered a modest nest egg of, say, $20,000, they would be entitled to no help whatsoever from Medicaid. They would have to spend it all on health care and become indigent in order to get help from the government. This would, in effect, force them into becoming their own (and your) worst nightmare— a burden to their kids, to society, and to everyone else.

If they squandered all their money on cha-cha lessons or managed to give it away to you and yours over the years, they can rest assured that they will probably be able to get Medicaid and stay home and functional as long as possible. If they were lousy, drunken child abusers who never worked an honest day in their lives, they can rest assured that their old age will be a comfortable one.

Medi*care*, on the other hand, is pretty useless in terms of any kind of long-term care or even at-home help. Eventually, of course, if your folks have not planned well, they will go through all their money in health care and will have nothing left to leave their children and grandchildren (that would be you and yours). So your father and your brother don't have to do anything, and you in turn get nothing. That's what they meant when they said, "Life ain't fair."

Anyway, the goal, no matter what the circumstances, is to keep your parents in their own home and functional as long as possible. First, however, you must honestly assess the situation. We hope you won't wait until it's too late and your parents are as functional as lettuce. We also hope they have done creative money management and don't have enough in the bank to require the government to make sure they get good and poor before it will help out. The law allows, by the way, for anyone to give (tax-free) anyone else $10,000 a year, which is what many people start doing well before they are incapacitated. That way, their children won't be burdened with them, and the system can't take from them what they've worked so hard for so long to make. You and/or your parents should talk to an accountant about all this ASAP.

Interestingly, the only person financially responsible for a parent is a spouse. Therefore, even if you are loaded, the government can't attack your money to pay for your parents' care.

This holds true, also, for any living wills they sign. They

may not even be valid from one state to another. If they do not want to linger on a machine, it's important that you all sit down now with an attorney and discuss it all rationally—and legally. Please. You won't regret it, but you might if you don't.

Ask the attorney, too, about medigap insurance (it fills in the gaps for Medicare and is being pushed like crazy by the AARP) and long-term-care insurance. You may be a day late and a dollar short on this one if your parents are already sickly.

Look into the health care proxy laws. You choose a health care proxy—a friend or relative—whom you trust to carry out the *spirit* of your wishes should you be unable to do so yourself. For example, you may want to be kept alive if there is even the slimmest chance of coming out of a coma, but not kept alive if there is not.

ASSESSING THE SITUATION AND THE OPTIONS

Keeping your folks comfortably in their own home is the real goal. It might be as simple as finding someone who will stop by every day to see if they need anything, from buying eggs to moving a chair. It's easy enough to get suggestions by asking around. If you live near your parents and have someone who helps out in your house, ask if he or she is available to help your parents on a limited daily basis.

If you have any influence whatsoever with your folks, try to get them to join support groups, senior centers, aerobics,

Gray Panthers, leisure clubs, the wonderful Meals On Wheels program. Even the dreaded bingo and cards can be tons of fun. They, like you, need company. They, like you, need to be stimulated. They, unlike you, don't need as much sex.

Here are some places to call for information:

Eldercare Locator (800-677-1116). Helps children of the elderly to find meal programs, transportation, housing, recreation, home-care attendants, nursing homes, and senior citizen centers.

National Academy of Elder Law Attorneys (520-881-4005). Referral for help with medical insurance and finances of the elderly.

National Family Caregivers Association (301-942-6430). Maintains a support network for children of elderly parents.

In the second stage of officially being old, your parents might require a companion. Don't panic. This won't necessarily be as expensive as it sounds. For one thing (and don't say we said it), there is a very large nontaxable working base in this country. These are people who are not on the tax rolls and who do child and elderly care for minimum wage. Very often, these people are new to this country and need a place to live and will be thrilled to live in with your parents. Just don't ever run for attorney general.

How do you find someone who is reliable, honest, and kind and who will not kill your parents in their sleep? The same way you found a reliable, honest, kind sitter for your kids while you worked. You asked everyone you knew for help, suggestions, recommendations, and the rest. Go find the person who took care of your kids while you were at work.

Recently the Clinton administration got involved with trying to figure out who's minding Mama. Reforms are in the works to monitor home health care aids more carefully. Or should we say, just carefully period?

At-home health care has become the major trend in long-term care, and the giant surge has created an almost limitless need for help—and limitless openings for unqualified help.

But remember, unless your parents are frail and suffering from Alzheimer's, they aren't helpless children who are at the mercy of a sitter. They can speak up, and they can certainly complain to you. And they will. Count on it. Don't treat them as if they are helpless if they aren't. They will probably drive anyone who cares for them nuts just like they drove you nuts. But at least, for the time being, you haven't reached critical mass.

What you all need at this stage is to find someone with common sense who can run a household. Period. Okay, that sounds doable, right? Right. The best recommendation comes from people you know. Period.

If your parents are frail but of sound mind, they will be

able to direct the housekeeper, and it's the best of all possible worlds.

However, if your parents are getting more fragile in mind and body with each passing day, it's important that the person who helps them out is in fact of sound mind and body himself or herself. Appearances can be deceiving. Ask questions. If a past job was, for example, a New York City cab driver, you should pass on him or her as a sane potential caretaker.

In the aging game, *USA Today* found that caretakers abused and stole from patients in every region of the country, maybe because almost 40 percent of the abusers and thieves had a criminal record or a history of abuse. God bless America!

Fifteen states now require background checks on caregivers, and soon all at-home caregivers will be under federal guidelines. That's good and it stinks. It means that they will charge at least minimum wage (plus agency fees) and will have to have taxes and social security taken out, which will make it too expensive to afford in most cases.

What you will get for the extra money is still not really clear other than the agency's assurance that person isn't a recently released serial killer. And you thought your worries were over when your kids were finally old enough to stay on their own without a sitter!

Okay, so you find the perfect affordable housekeeper for your parents. Now you have another thing to think about: the seventh day when the housekeeper takes off. Hey, even

God took a rest. Figure out what you will do for coverage that day.

Well, if you live within a hundred miles of your parents, it won't kill you to visit them once a week. In fact, it's the least you can do. If you don't, you or they will have to buy coverage for that day.

Invest in a medical alert device, which costs around $300 and is worn around the neck at all times. If they've fallen and they can't get up, they can press the button, and the medics will come a-running. It will save all concerned many nights' sleep.

But suppose your parents are no longer able to live on their own. What are the alternatives? The big *n* word lingers in the air like a bad stink: nursing home!

Remember *Where's Poppa?* with George Segal? "We have to put Mama in a nnnnnnnnnnnnuuuuurrrr . . ." Uttering these words would immediately render him helpless— mentally, physically, and sexually. It was funny then; it has a nightmare ring of truth now.

But wait. There *are* alternatives to nursing homes. The new thing on the horizon is called senior homes. This is a brilliant idea, especially if your parents have a home to sell and can afford the cost of a senior home.

These homes (often condolike apartments) are care-based and physical need–based communities. Even the big hotel chains are beginning to get into the senior housing business.

A person who is physically able to care for himself or herself will live in an apartment, with meals shared in a restaurant-type dining room. There is a full-time staff including health care workers. Residents can cook for themselves at home if they don't want the company. There is a gradually increasing health care progression, with more care given as required. When and if residents need it, they can be moved into a full-care twenty-four-hour-a-day facility within the complex.

They are equipped with emergency pull cords which, when activated, will alert EMS techs, who will be there within ten minutes.

The cheaper and oftentimes better alternative to senior homes is real homes that are licensed by the state. There are people out there who perhaps have grown children and big houses to pay for, so they open their homes to two to four seniors. The seniors live generally in the bosom of a hodge-podge family made up of themselves and any members of the family who live in the house. In the experience of some of our friends, these homes are cheaper than nursing homes and generally much more pleasant. Contact your state agency on aging to find out where there are these kinds of places in your area.

There is a horrible catch to these homes in many states, though. Again, a cruel catch created by idiot government bureaucrats. The elderly person must be completely ambulatory to stay in the home. Therefore, if your parents get cozy in this home, are happy, and you have peace of mind, it can all come to an end if they fall or when they can no longer get around by themselves for whatever reason. The state will simply not allow the elderly residents to remain.

What all of this comes to is that you really need to do the awful deed before it's too late: See a lawyer and an accountant together. Be sure you discuss legal, moral, and financial issues thoroughly with your folks before it's too late.

With any luck, everyone can make known his or her wishes without everyone fighting and accusing everyone else of horrible things. Good luck.

NURSING HOMES

Should the dreaded moment come, be prepared. Worst-case scenario: Your parent is in the hospital suffering from a totally debilitating stroke or heart attack and cannot return home. Ever.

Just when you think it can't get any worse, it does. When Rosemary's mother was in the hospital after a massive stroke, the hospital kept pressuring her to get her mother out. She and her sister had to decide instantly on a nursing home, something they had successfully put out of their minds until this second. The truth is that one of the horrors of managed care, HMOs, and other network health systems is that hospitals will tell you right off the bat to get a list of five nursing homes. And the one with the first opening is the one selected. It will not matter to the hospital that the only home with openings is run by disgruntled workers who have a better record for neglect than for care.

This means that you have to run around scouting out

nursing homes while your sick and incapacitated parent lies in the hospital. As surreal as that is, you'll find that nursing homes simultaneously hustle you ("We're the best") and then have the balls to tell you that there are no rooms—and a ten-year waiting list!

A little secret: The worse off your parents are, the more care they require, and the less money they have, the quicker they will move to the top of the list. In fact, when they are in this condition and the state is footing the bill, they're in as soon as anybody in the joint kicks the bucket. Oy!

The only solution—and it stinks, too—is to check out homes (without your parents) before you have to and pick out the best. Do this by interviewing the admissions people and know before you *need* to know your options. It's horrible enough to have to put your parent in a home. The best you can hope for at this stage is to know your options and to know what you are doing before it all breaks down into uncontrollable hysteria.

twenty-three

Fallen Idols

WIVES WE WANTED TO BE

In a galaxy long, long ago and far away, we dreamed of
marrying well for a living. If you couldn't marry *well*, well,
at least you could marry.

CAN YOU BELIEVE WE EVER WANTED TO BE

- **Connie Stevens**
  She married Eddie Fisher. (And we thought *we*
  married losers!)

- **Elizabeth Taylor**

  She married Eddie Fisher *and* Larry Fortensky!

- **Jane Fonda**

  Actress turned activist turned exercise guru turned
  trophy wife/beefalo booster.

CAN YOU BELIEVE WE EVER ENVIED

- **Linda Eastman McCarthy**

  She landed the cute Beatle and went on to be the
  Lucy Ricardo of rock and roll.

- **Yoko Ono**

  She landed the brilliant Beatle and went on to be
  the Lucy Ricardo of rock and roll.

- **Princess Grace**

  Academy award–winning actress turned princess
  of two-bit country.

- **Priscilla Presley**

  She married the king only to have her daughter
  marry the queen.

HUSBANDS WE WANTED TO HAVE

In an entirely different galaxy, long, long ago and very far
away, we always dreamed that the perfect husband could be
ours if we were just thinner, hipper, richer, cuter.

CAN YOU BELIEVE WE EVER WANTED TO MARRY

- **JFK**

  He was young, he was hot, he was the president who couldn't keep it in his pants. Why does that sound familiar?

- **Marlon Brando**

  He was young, he was hot, he was recently photographed in the largest recorded adult diaper.

- **Elvis Presley**

  He was young, he was hot, he went on to dress like Liberace in sausage casing.

- **Jim Morrison**

  He was young, he was hot, he wound up with a sixty-four-inch waist.

- **Paul McCartney**

  He was young, he was hot, he grew up to be Angela Lansbury.

DREAM BOYFRIENDS

CAN YOU BELIEVE WE WERE EVER IN LOVE WITH

- **Edd "Kookie" Byrnes**
- **Richard "Dr. Kildaire" Chamberlain**
- **Vince "Dr. Ben Casey" Edwards**
- **Tony "Beaver's Brother" Dow**
- **Troy "Parrish" Donahue**

- Fabian "Like a Tiger" Forte
- Mickey "the Monkee" Dolenz
- Ricky "Teenage Idol" Nelson
- Burt "Rug" Reynolds
- Clint "Rawhide" Eastwood

  Hey, wait a minute, we're still in love with him!

Money: A Guide for the Fiscally Impaired

No Money, No Funny.
—Anonymous

We've said it before and we'll say it again: If only we had spent the early part of our lives reading *The Prince* instead of waiting for him, we'd now be a little more comfortable in the world of money and business, not to mention Lexus dealerships.

Like it or not, knowing about money is essential for us all, since at some point in our lives, nine out of ten women in this country will be responsible for their own finances. So if we don't want to spend our twilight years dining on Friskies Buffet, we have to learn about dough. Fast.

What follows is a simple guide for the fiscally impaired. If you are filthy rich, have an MBA, or marry well for a living, you can move on to the next chapter.

Oh, you're still with us? Okay.

RETIREMENT

Planning for retirement would be simple if we only knew exactly when we were going to die. But since most of us don't know our actual checkout time, this means we have to have a plan.

The word "retirement" does not exactly roll off the average baby boomer tongue because we are the generation that considered Peter Pan an old man.

And since women earn less than men—20 percent less—we have smaller savings, pensions, and Social Security coming to us when we retire. And since we live longer than men, we need *more*, not less, money at retirement. Equate that one.

Every seven seconds another baby boomer turns fifty and wonders if it is possible to retire in thirty years, let alone fifteen. Of course, you won't have any problem if you never had kids, ate out, took a vacation, or bought anything that wasn't designed for Kmart.

Don't despair. There are lots of things you can do, starting right now. But start.

- Save, save, save. If it doesn't hurt, you're not saving enough. Americans save less than citizens of most other industrial nations who are taxed much higher. Living in the moment is, of course, part of the American way, and since baby boomers practically invented instant gratification, we have notoriously been a generation of spenders, not savers.

- Consume less. Cut back on your living expenses by 10 percent, starting this year. Use both ends of the Q-Tip. Stop shopping as a leisure-time activity. It used to be a necessity. Remember? Look in your closets and your junk drawers. You have enough stuff. When you were young, you thought middle-class acquisitions were decadent and bourgeois. Right? Well, start thinking that way again. You must repeat the following like a mantra. Zen saying: "You have everything you need." Authors' saying: "Don't buy any more crap!"

- Get rid of all your credit cards except one. Boomers are notorious credit card junkies. Right now consumer debt is $1.2 trillion and that's an after-tax, nondeductible, stress-laden trillion. Go cold turkey and get out of debt.

- Get a financial adviser. He or she will take you seriously because American women earned *$1 trillion* in 1995. Woof.

- Invest, invest, invest. This doesn't mean go the old maid route with a 3 percent passbook account or go wild with get-rich-quick stocks with a 20 percent-plus return. In short, don't get panicky and don't be piggy. Frankly, if you were a pro, you wouldn't be reading this.

- Then reinvest. Automatically reinvest all the money you make so you never get your greedy mitts on it.
- Buy retirement planning software. Then hide it. Recommended is Quicken Financial Planner (800-446-8848) and the T. Rowe Price Retirement Planning Kit (800-638-5660).
- Do a budget. We hate to be the ones saying this, but you gotta face the facts.
- Track inflation. To give you an idea of how voracious inflation is, just remember that when you were in high school—in *this* century—a luxury car cost $2,800 and a postage stamp was only 5 cents!
- Teach your kids about fiscal responsibility. Especially when it comes to the novel idea of supporting themselves. If not, they will be living with you until they are forty-six.
- You don't have to retire at sixty-five. Boomer babes will survive longer than any previous generation of women. That sounds great, but it means we'll need more money than any previous generation of women, too. If you keep working, remember never to let the heels of your shoes get run down. If you do, people will know you're working because you need the dough and not the intellectual stimulation.
- Assume you will have a part-time job or volunteer work after you retire. It's better for both your psyche

and your pocketbook. You may not believe it the next time you drag yourself to work on a rainy day, but the most common complaint among retirees is boredom. After all, how many times can you watch *Where the Boys Are?*

- Never go to a luau. They are expensive, fattening, and the hula is humiliating at any age.

SOCIAL SECURITY: THE IMPOSSIBLE DREAM?

Retirement is actually a twentieth-century invention. People used to work until they dropped dead. When Social Security was started in 1935, many thought of it as a Bolshevik plot. The feds picked sixty-five as retirement age, confident in the knowledge that the average life span was only sixty-two years. Now it is seventy-six and counting. And, as we know, there are lots of baby boomers planning to drop out one last time and head into that retirement commune. This smells like the beginnings of a crisis, what economists are now calling "social insecurity."

Right now, there are three workers plugging money into the Social Security trust fund for every one retiree. By the time the first boomers retire in 2011, there will be only two workers for each retiree. It is predicted that unless the system changes, the Social Security trust fund will be depleted by 2029.

If we're pissed off at the previous generation for living so long, how will these Generation X'ers feel when they realize they're subsidizing the retirement of the biggest generation of oldsters in American history? Fortunately they're still only twenty-something and haven't figured that out yet, but when they do, they'll probably round us up and shoot us.

Don't get your underwear in a bunch just yet. Solutions that might work:

- Raise the retirement age. President Reagan, who knew a thing or two about old age, already raised the retirement age: By 2009, it will be sixty-six and by 2027, it will be sixty-seven.
- Shift Medicare over to managed care.

All the problems with social security will be over when we baby boomers have all died away. Then the proportion between the young and the old will be leveled off, since the pig in the python has moved to the big sty in the sky.

WHAT'S YOUR SOCIAL SECURITY STASH?

You can actually get an accounting of how much Social Security money you have in your account. Call up this twenty-four-hour number, 1-800-772-1213, for a form called Request for Earnings and Benefit Estimate Statement.

INVESTING

Virginia Morris, author of *A Woman's Guide to Investing*, offers this wonderful quote: "Investing is a lot like exercise:

You may have to talk yourself into starting." And the first step is to educate yourself, so here goes.

THE STOCK MARKET

The stock market used to be for rich, old Republican guys who sat around at their clubs in leather chairs. It was front-page news when a ladies' bathroom was installed at the Stock Exchange.

The baby boom generation brought the middle class to the stock market: *The New York Times* recently reported that 40 percent of all middle-class Americans now invest in the stock market. The market has been booming thanks to boomers who keep the money surging with their retirement funds.

We are in the fourteenth year—1987 notwithstanding—of the greatest sustained bull market in history. This begs the following questions: Is it too late to get in since stock prices are now at nosebleed levels? Should we put more in and be part of the next big ride? Should we pull all our dough out now before it crashes down to earth? What's a girl to do?

That depends on whether you need some quick cash for a chin implant or something equally urgent.

Women, whether they know it or not, have all the qualities that make great investors. They aren't afraid to ask questions or admit they are confused, and they are open to advice. They're more concerned with meeting goals than making a killing. Let's be frank, we're not constantly mea-

suring our unit against the next guy's. We just have to remember we have the right stuff to be investors.

Here's a guide that won't land you in a leather chair at the
club with a cigar hanging out of your mouth, but it might
prevent you from being a seventy-four-year-old waitress
standing all day in beige orthopedic shoes in a job that is hell
on your varicose veins.

- Buy low and sell high. Duh.
- Get a broker. We suggest that you think of a broker
  like a gynecologist—you should be able to talk to
  her, ask her questions, and trust her.
- Pay as you go. This means open a cash account with
  your broker. The alternative, margin account, means
  you borrow as you go and the firm can sell without
  notice to you. Margin accounts are the jump-out-
  the-window kind.
- The older you are—that means you—the more you
  should invest in bigger, solid companies. Leave the
  heady growth funds to the twentysomethings with
  their twentysomething bowels. They have more time
  to recoup.
- Be educated. Buy stock in companies you understand. You don't need to track the Dow Jones Industrial Average daily to be successful (thank God).
- Ask yourself how much you can afford to lose. Let's
  keep it simple: If your investments are keeping you
  up all night, get out of the market. At your age, you
  need your sleep.

- Be prepared to sit it out if your stock dips. The market must, as it's euphemistically called, correct itself from time to time. At press time the market was still reeling from one such "correction." Reeling but rebounding.
- Monitor your investments. Keep your monthly statements and confirmation slips.
- Don't load up on your company stock, thinking that your employer will like you better. If you get fired, chances are it's because your company is doing badly, and that means your stock is, too.
- Beware of on-line investment scams. If it sounds too good to be true, it is.
- Stay away from futures and options—unless, of course, you have a lifetime supply of Maalox and rich relatives.

MUTUAL FUNDS

Most of the boomer money in the stock market is there via mutual funds since, with the largest bull market in history going on, amateur investors have realized that they don't need an expert to help them pick stocks. Mutual funds have grown by $2.5 trillion in just four years. You don't need much dough to open one, your money stays liquid, and professional money managers do the research for you. Mutual funds are not insured by a bank or federal agency.

Here are some guidelines to mutual funds.

- Shop around. Compare different funds.
- Diversify. Don't limit yourself to one type of mutual fund. Experts suggest that six to twelve mutual funds is a good idea. Have no more than 10 percent of your portfolio in a single fund.
- Look for no-load funds. No-load means no-commission.
- Buyer beware: Past performance is not a reliable indicator of future performance.
- Know what you want. Are you looking for growth or income or both? (Hint: At your age, you should be looking more for income.)
- Reinvest. Rule: The higher the rate of return, the higher the risk of loss.

INDEX FUNDS

Index funds are mutual funds that mirror a market index or maybe even a whole market. Basically this means that you can own a piece of everything. The best broad market index is called the Standard & Poor's 500 (an unfortunate name, considering their line of work).

BONDS

Rule: The closer you are to gumming your food, the more you should invest in bonds.

A bond is an IOU from a company or the government to you. In exchange for borrowing your money, it promises to pay back your principal with interest. Interesting note: Government agency bonds, for reasons known only to some jokester at the Fed, all have hillbilly names—Ginnie Mae, Freddie Mac, and Fannie Mae. Go figure.

RETIREMENT ACCOUNTS

401(K)

During the last decade employers have been favoring 401(k) plans over the traditional pension plans. These are a really good deal. It's a tax-deferred nest egg for about twenty-four million Americans, and right now, the total of this particular nest egg is $675 billion.

But the real beauty of a 401(k) is this: Since your contribution is in pretax dollars, the amount of your gross income reported to the IRS is less. You save on your tax bill and you save for retirement at the same time.

So, if you're lucky enough to have one, max out on your 401(k).

Fawn over the person in your office who manages the fund, bring him or her cappuccino every morning. You have no secrets from this person since he or she already knows both your salary and age, and this is a relationship that could be important to your future.

IRA

You can and should make a $2,000 annual contribution to a tax-deferred IRA account, which will compound interest until you retire at age sixty-five. If you're married and your husband doesn't work—sorry about that—you can create a "spousal IRA," thereby setting aside $4,000 a year. Or your husband can do it for you if you don't work—and by the way, how did you pull *that* off?

Baby boomers are the most mobile work force in history (probably because we're always pissed off about something). If you're thinking of switching employers, find out if you are sacrificing any of your pension benefits and factor that into your decision.

Semi-interesting note: IRAs are named after Ira Cohen, an IRS actuary. This piece of information is of no use whatsoever.

KEOGH

People who qualify for Keogh plans: small-business owners, the self-employed, someone who sits on a board of directors (as if he needs the money), and anyone who works as a freelancer. The paperwork is so bad that even accountants have to hire someone to do it for them.

ANNUITIES

An annuity is a contract from an insurance company to pay you an amount of money for a specified period of time or as long as you live. When you learn about annuities, all you can remember is Woody Allen's line about how he now believes in hell since he spent an evening with an insurance agent.

INSURANCE

A general note on insurance: The older you become, the more self-sufficient your kids become—we hope. This means you can reduce and eventually eliminate your life insurance.

Disability insurance: Now is the time to start seriously thinking about disability insurance since it's harder to get the older you get and much more expensive for women. (That's because statistics show that more women get disabled more often than men.) Remember that health insurance is responsible only for medical bills and won't replace the salary you lose if you're out of work for an extended period. A good disability policy should be about 60 percent of your full salary. This is a must.

Medical insurance: One of the things that you'll find out when you get older is that medical costs skyrocket. That's why God and Lyndon B. Johnson invented Medicare. You can't collect Medicare until you are sixty-five, so in the meantime remember these essentials:

- Keep covered. You really have no choice unless Socialists take over the government.
- Pay premiums on time.
- If you're married, determine who has the better policy and go with it.
- Make sure your kids are insured, even if they're over twenty-three.
- Find out what happens to your insurance if you are divorced or widowed.

A CLOSING NOTE

Arthur Levitt Jr., former head of the American Stock Exchange and current chairman of the SEC, offers these words of advice for women planning their financial future: "Just learn to take care of yourself." To which we add: "Because odds are nobody else is going to."

twenty-five

Life: When Bad Things Happen to Good Babes

DOWNSIZED! (OR, AS IT USED TO BE CALLED, SHITCANNED!)

Downsized is just a fancy word for being out of a job. Whether you're the president of a major corporation or the person who cleans up after the elephants in the circus, getting your walking papers hurts. At first. However, many of the women we've spoken to found that a career change in midlife was the best thing that ever happened to them.

F. Scott Fitzgerald may have said that there are no second acts in American lives, but we prefer to follow the words of that great sage, Yogi Berra, who said, "It ain't over till it's over." And women of the baby boom generation are starting over all over the place. Women bankers are becoming astrologers, single Welfare moms are going to Congress, lawyers are becoming Buddhist nuns, and strippers are becoming lawyers.

So take heart. But there are a few things you should do and not do when your boss says not to let the door hit you on the ass on your way out.

- Don't panic. Instead, size up the situation. Determine how long you can go without a job. Should you stay in your field, train for a new career, or just go get your nails done?
- Talk to the benefits person in your office, that person you've been bringing cappuccino to. Get the poop on your pension and medical insurance.
- Put your emotions aside and ask yourself if you have been canned for "just cause." If you think you've been treated unfairly, talk to a lawyer.
- Live without an alarm clock up your keister. If you can swing it, now is the time to do things you've been putting off: going back to school, taking a road trip, going to daytime baseball games with your kids, planting a garden, and even cleaning out your closets. (Well, maybe cleaning out the closets is a bit drastic.)
- Don't stay in your jammies and watch daytime TV. It's demoralizing and will make you feel like a loser.

DIVORCE

Fact: There's about a 47 percent chance that you'll get—or have already gotten—a divorce. Women of our generation revolutionized the image of the neighborhood divorced lady. We don't walk around in toreador pants and backless heels with pom-poms on the toes looking to steal somebody's husband. Well, not *all* the time. We take care of ourselves, but even in today's postrevolutionary times, women still lose out economically with divorce. While it's usually a good idea to throw the bum out (providing he *is* a bum), here are some things to remember:

- Get professional advice and get it immediately. You can be sure *he* already has. Know your debt liability, especially when it comes to the IRS.
- Establish your own credit and checking account ASAP.
- Freeze your joint investment accounts.
- Change your will.
- If you're thinking of alimony and have been married less than fifteen years, don't spend the money quite yet. That's because you may not get any.
- Don't let it drag on and avoid going to court. Both are expensive and, worse, hell on a babe's mental health and looks.

THE GOOD NEWS

- Child support payments are easier to enforce. Finally.

- The depression you go through will probably cause you to lose fifteen pounds.

- When you adjust—and you will—you'll probably slowly find yourself rejoicing! Yes! Yes! No more socks on the floor, wet towels on the bed, or him glued to the tube.

- Know that he will be miserable. His young girlfriend will leave him, and he will be just another old guy with hair in his ears.

- You can take a lover. Or four.

- You are young enough to date like crazy. And you're old enough not to *need* to.

- The next man you have dinner with will actually look at you when he speaks. And more shocking, he will actually *speak*.

- You can spend Saturdays getting a bikini wax instead of hanging out at Home Depot.

WIDOWHOOD

Since a good man is hard to find, it really stinks when he dies. But the odds are that you will outlive your husband by fifteen years. Make a lot of the so-called death arrangements while both of you can still do the macarena. Here's a brief guide:

- Don't make any major decision in the first six months. Don't throw anything out either.
- Don't isolate. See your friends, your neighbors, even second cousins you haven't seen for years. People want to help. Let them know you're okay, can talk about your loss, and will not start wailing in public.
- Take care of business. It will keep you busy, and there are some things you *must* take care of—like transferring all bank accounts, real estate, and brokerage accounts to your name. If your husband had a pension, ask the custodian about survivor annuity.
- Find out what debts you are liable for. Remember, the most important is the IRS, because they are the meanest creditors on earth.

WHEN YOUR NUMBER COMES UP

While you don't necessarily have to get old, you will, at some point, have to die. So put a clothespin on your nose and start planning for it. You must, because even if you're poor, you don't want the government to get its mitts on your original LP of "Sgt. Pepper's Lonely Hearts Club Band," do you?

It's all very complicated and boring and depressing. Here's what you must do:

- Find a good estate planning attorney. If you don't have a recommendation, you can call the Estate Planning Specialists at 800-223-9610.

- Get a power of attorney document. This will give a family member or close friend legal authority to act in your behalf in case you get so incapacitated that you don't even know you're wearing diapers.
- Express your wishes regarding the disposition of your, shall we say, remains.
- Set up a will. Indicate who's in charge of your financial affairs and who gets what and who will handle the distribution of your assets. This should not be someone who knows, or even looks like, Kato Kaelin.
- Get a living will. This states that you don't—or do—want to be kept alive by life-support systems if you are seriously ill and cannot communicate. Another option is to appoint a health care proxy who will make health choices for you if you are unconscious. An attorney will tell you, with a perfectly straight face, not to choose your main beneficiary as health care proxy.
- Learn how to avoid estate taxes. They are immense and you would probably drop dead from the amount if you weren't already dead. You are liable for these in the event that your estate is over $1 million, and it's unlikely that your survivors will be able to convince Sotheby's to have an auction of your faux pearls to help pay the tax bill. Some tips:
  —Transfer dough to your husband (that is, if you're speaking to him). This is having all

your assets in "joint tenancy with rights of survivorship" or "unlimited marital deduction." Make sure he doesn't secretly have a seventeen-year-old girlfriend.

—If you're rich—and we hope you are—give $10,000 per year (if you're single) and $20,000 (if you're married) to any and all deserving friends and relatives. Your estate will save on taxes and people will say nice things about you *before* you die.

—Set up an A-B trust if you're married. The A part of the trust is what goes to your husband when you die, and the B part goes to children and grandchildren when he dies.

One tip before you head for the last roundup. Think about setting up a trust for your beneficiaries while you're still alive. This is called, not surprisingly, a living trust. Transfer some of your assets into a trust, and you or a manager will distribute them to your beneficiaries. The trust, not your beneficiaries, will pay taxes on the income it generates. When you die, your family will be spared the pain of probate. Besides delays, time-consuming hassles, and high attorney fees, probate is public! Which means that when you are dead and buried, anyone and everyone can look at your will and either laugh, tsk-tsk, or say "that bitch!"

twenty-six

Help! It's the AARP Envelope
in the Mailbox

It comes whether you want it to or not. It knows where you live, and it finds you before you find it. It even comes before it's due.

Tragically, months before you turn the dreaded *f* word, you look in your mailbox and there it is in all it's glossy horror—*Modern Maturity.* Yes, it's the AARP magazine greeting you with a cheery, "Welcome." Welcome?! Goat droppings in the mailbox would be more welcome.

You've got a better chance of winning lotto two times in a row than you have of getting off—or better yet, never getting put on—the AARP mailing list. They're bold and they're old! And now they claim, in theory at least, that they want you to join their club. Talk about not wanting to join any club that would have you for a member. Don't they know that we boomer babes are too cool for the AARP?

The bad news is that there is nothing—repeat, nothing— you can do about it. The good news is that should you desire to stay at the Red Roof Inn at some point in what remains of your life, you can now get an AARP discount.

And once they find you and it starts, they are more persistent than a Jehovah's Witness with a quota.

But please be warned. This is not just a benign envelope delivered to your door. It's literally a letter bomb that can destroy life as you know it.

You're a made babe, as they say in newspapers and other organized crime syndicates, when the very first piece of mail arrives.

For one thing, the mail carrier for sure knows a huge truth about you now—your age. You're not thirty-five, and now an employee of the U.S. Postal Service knows it. Right off it ups the mailman Christmas gift ante by at least another ten, maybe twenty bucks, depending on your geographical location.

You can run, babe, but you can't hide, not from the AARP age police.

Take Linda's sad story. Please.

Her mailman, Gary Goldberg, was warned that should that thing ever arrive, he was to throw it into the trash, no questions asked. Instead, his psycho killer instincts took over. He not only had the doorman phone up to say an important piece of mail was waiting downstairs, he circled the AARP logo—and then laughed out loud. There was really no way of convincing him or anyone else that the envelope was a full twelve months early.

If, God forbid, your mailman is anything like Gary, you're a dead woman.

But really, it doesn't matter. The AARP wants you to get caught. Sooner or later your neighbors are bound to catch you sneaking the envelope out of the mailbox. In a few seconds you've aged decades in their eyes.

Then there's that other unspeakable dilemma: What if the man you're living with thinks he's older than you and picks up the mail first? Quicker than you can add forty-five and five, you will take on Aunt Bee qualities in his eyes. Why didn't he ever think to buy you a nice housecoat or lace-up brown shoes, he thinks, while attempting to make eye contact with a toots who wasn't born when John Lennon was shot.

It's a dreadful situation.

Who are these AARP people and who appointed them the official age police? Why do they take it upon themselves to taunt you about turning fifty? After you've been lying about your age for years, how do they know the truth? Is there a conspiracy between the federal government and these bounty age hunters?

We set out to find the truth for ourselves by going to the

source—the AARP headquarters building in Washington, D.C. We haven't felt this much rage in D.C. since the March on Washington in 1968.

There it stood, the grandest building in Washington aside from the White House. It sits diagonally across the street from the Securities and Exchange Commission building. The AARP building makes the SEC building look like it's on welfare. (The SEC is only the governmental body that regulates the stock market!)

The AARP building's got gold trim. It's got a big atrium. It's got marble halls. It's got lots and lots of floors. Everyone who works there looks like he or she got dressed in 1962. The women wear slips and girdles—even the twenty-five-year-olds. Their behinds look square. Their modest suits cover their knees. They speak in quiet tones. Boomer babes do not exist here.

There are something like two thousand employees. There are something like thirty million members. The AARPeople say they are hoping to nail at least half of us—the seventy million upcoming boomers. But after visiting the place, we feel sure that they only want to torture us with their literature. They want our money, but they don't want us. There seems to be an underlying fear that boomers will come in and start taking over, holding sit-ins in the president's office until they force them into open enrollments and insisting that lobbying efforts are geared toward the legalization of pot. Damn young whippersnappers!

Here's how it went down when we went down. The February day we boarded the Metroliner was deceptively warm. Unfortunately, it was one of the few days that the Metroliner didn't derail. After making sure that no one was following us, we slunk into the lobby. There were guards. What can they possibly think anyone would want to steal? Past issues of *Modern Maturity*? Perhaps they fear that marauding bands of Gray Panthers will break in and rape and rampage on the medigap floor.

Our first appointment was with Dr. Margaret Dixon, a seventy-four-year-old former New York City school principal. She is a lovely woman who is everything you believe a seventy-four-year-old former New York City school principal should be. We talked to her for an hour. We were here and we wanted answers!

Q: Dr. Dixon, how does the AARP find you no matter what?

A: Well, it's a little of this and a little of that. You know, it's lots of research. If you could fax me the question, I'll get right back to you on that.

Q: Dr. Dixon, how do you avoid making the list in the first place?

A: Tee-hee, giggle giggle. You girls sure are funny.

Q: Okay, then, Dr. Dixon, how do you get off the list?

A: Why would you want to? If you fax me the question, I'll try to find that out for you. No one's ever asked that question before. Aging is not what aging used to be, though, I'll tell you that. We want to bring a new perspective to the concept of aging.

She did, too. "If you don't want to turn fifty, just die at forty-nine."

We next met with the Communications Director, James R. Holland.

Q: Mr. Holland, how does the AARP find you no matter what?

A: Hahaha. We've got research upon research, we do. You know, driver's licenses and the like. But we protect those lists like the formula for original Coke.

Q: So if you never got a license, you wouldn't get on your list?

A: Well, I didn't say that now, did I?

Q: How do you get off the list?

A: I don't know, no one's ever asked me before. Maybe Tom Otwell can answer these questions for you.

Tom Otwell took over while Jim hightailed it out of there. The next thing you read is the most valuable bit of advice in the entire book. Clip it and put it inside your wallet.

Q: Mr. Otwell, how do you get off the AARP mailing list?

A: Well, I don't think anyone's ever asked me that question before. But I suppose if you didn't respond to our [AARP] mailings ever, after a while I guess we'd take you off the mailing list.

The AARP is huge. It knows more about you than the FBI did in 1967. It says it exists to make your life easier as you get older. That's not true.

How does the AARP figure it's easier? Say you break down and go for the $8 membership fee and get an AARP membership card. Say you then go to the movies, and the theater has a sign posted: "AARP discounts to seniors with membership card." Do you save the $3.50 and humiliate yourself showing it to the snotnose in the ticket booth, or do you keep that little sucker right in your wallet and spend the $3.50 extra for the full-fee ticket and feel cheated through the whole movie? It stinks!

Then there's the magazine. The only saving grace about receiving *Modern Maturity* that we can see is that every month they have a column called "The Big Five-Oh" and in it you get to see who's turned fifty so you don't feel so bad. The big January 1996 "Boo!mer" issue (yes, that's how it was written, and then they say they can't wait 'til we join!) showed Diane Keaton, Dolly Parton, and Tricia Cox. Of course, Tricia Cox was fifty when she was eighteen, so that didn't feel too comforting.

Anyway, if the AARP is the only club that's ever solicited you as a member, and you feel inclined to join, you will be let in on their lobbying efforts on your behalf as well as things like medigap insurance (covers the difference between what Medicare pays and the patient's portion) as well as discounts to hotels, movies, medicines, and trailer camps.

They talk a lot about their discount car insurance, but everyone we know (older than us, of course!) who's ever inquired about it reports back that it is more expensive by far than what they are currently paying. This is a surprise? What do you expect when you put yourself into the insurance pool of possibly the worst drivers in the world— eighty-five-year-olds! Have you ever driven in Florida? You could get killed standing still at a red light.

What they can offer you right now, however, is lots of advice about how to deal with your aging parents and how to plan for our retirement and so forth. There's even a Web site: AARP.ORG

Our advice? Burn the AARP mail like you did your bra and like you did your boyfriends' draft cards. It's the only way, really. If you don't, you are not a boomer babe and never will be. We're sorry, but you must stop reading this book. After all, your *Modern Maturity* has just arrived, and you don't want to miss the story on new senior villages in Arizona.

Strict? Sure, but somebody has to take charge here!

twenty-seven

Your Fiftieth Birthday:
It's Your Party, and You Can
Cry If You Want To

The time is coming up when you have to make one of the major decisions of your life: how (or if) to celebrate your fiftieth birthday.

Do you rent out Madison Square Garden like President Clinton, do you dress up as Marie Antoinette like Elton John, or do you eat a pint of Ben & Jerry's in a darkened bedroom like Celeste Fremont?

Even though you probably can't afford Madison Square Garden or an eighteenth-century wig and false mole, you *can* afford a pint of ice cream. But is that really the way to go?

You may have hidden during your fortieth and (if you're neurotic) your thirtieth, but, for some perverse reason, it makes sense to come out on your fiftieth. We haven't actually figured out what that reason is, but here are some considerations.

First of all, you're at an age where you shouldn't care what people think (unless they think you're a secret Scientologist).

Second, everyone has probably figured out that you're about fifty anyhow. (Is there really such a big difference between forty-eight and fifty? Answer: Yes, if you're forty-eight.)

Third, you can preempt that noxious question, "Have you turned fifty yet?"

Fourth, you'll get a better quality of birthday presents than ever before because most of your friends are old.

Fifth, you're still a babe.

Sixth, you haven't flipped out.

Celebrating your fiftieth with the people in your life is good, particularly because, well, for one thing, strangers wouldn't give you as nice presents.

Josie Natori, the designer, rented out Carnegie Hall for her fiftieth and played Schumann's Piano Concerto in A Minor for 2,800 of her nearest and dearest—and oh, yes, the press.

She laid out around half a mil for the party. Now we're not saying she should have given the money to poor children if she didn't want to, but, forcing 2,800 people to listen to her play classical music probably left her with 2,799 fewer nearest and dearest.

The president, as we said, played the Garden on his fiftieth, forgetting for a minute that he is not in fact JFK, who did the same once. Unfortunately Marilyn Monroe was long dead, so she couldn't make the gig to sing "Happy Birthday, Mr. President" while his humiliated wife skipped the party altogether.

What other things have real-life boomers done recently, now that one of us is turning the big 5-0 every seven seconds? One of our friends took his girlfriend and started out on a car trip the night before his fiftieth. His goal was to hit as many roller-coasters in one day as possible. First stop? An after-dark horrifying ride on the best coaster in America, the Cyclone, at Coney Island. They managed to hit seven coasters in the following twenty-four hours. The car ride rivaled the coasters for sheer terror, by the way.

Another friend took her teenage daughter and went whitewater rafting on the Colorado, sleeping out every night for a week.

Linda went swimming with the dolphins in Florida. Why? Because a good fin is hard to find. When she got back, her pals Rosemary and Stu threw her a surprise party, for which she will never forgive them. Of course it beat her fortieth, when Stu sent a terrible Dr. Ruth impersonator, a stripping cop, and a twelve-foot chicken to her birthday party in a New York City restaurant.

At press time, Rosemary was living in hellish fear that the same fate would befall her. Stay tuned.

Another friend's boyfriend signed her up for motorcycle classes and bought her a Harley.

What'll you do? With any luck, it will be something you've never had the nerve to do before. What do you have to lose? (Besides your life, we mean.)

Hey—as movie producer Frank Marshall said after being hoisted mosh-pit style and then forcing Hollywood honchos to watch him do magic tricks the night of his fiftieth, "You're only fifty once." Unless of course, you, like Albert Einstein, believe in quantum physics, in which case you are fifty hundreds of times in the space-time continuum. Once is probably enough.

Whatever you do, though, go out in grand style! We expect nothing less. And, oh yeah . . . Happy Birthday Babe!

FIFTY GREAT WAYS TO TURN FIFTY

1. Rent out Madison Square Garden, like our boy Bill, then charge people to come and call it a fund-raiser.
2. Get tanked with your girlfriends.
3. Do something you've always wished you had the nerve to do. You'll be forgiven—it's your birthday and people expect you to be temporarily insane.
4. Grab your best friend and drive Route 66, stopping at every nutty place on the road.

5. Go visit the country your family is from and find your long lost relatives.

6. Spa yourself.

7. Go blond, if you aren't already. If you are, go red.

8. Give up smoking and take up meditating.

9. Find and call your high school boyfriend.

10. Find and call your college boyfriend.

11. Find and call your best friend from elementary school.

12. Go white-water rafting on the Colorado River in Utah. Wake up in the middle of the night in your tent and go out and look up. That's all we'll tell you—just look up.

13. Tell your parents you love them.

14. Tell your children you love them more than life itself.

15. Stay in bed with your husband or your lover for twenty-four hours.

16. Visit a psychic.

17. Call in sick. For two weeks.

18. Start running with the goal of entering a mini-marathon by your fifty-first birthday. (Rosemary runs 'em all the time.)

19. Call your husband, lover, whatever at work and say, "You thrill me."

20. Sign up for a life drawing class.

21. Get a total makeover.

22. Give yourself a party and make everyone come dressed as his or her high school yearbook photo. (They must bring their real pics.)

23. Start to write your book. (You know you want to!)
24. Swim naked.
25. Visit Roswell.
26. Rent a convertible and drive with the top down, even if it's the dead of winter. Especially if it's the dead of winter.
27. Climb a mountain. Ski it if you've never skied before.
28. Take flying lessons.
29. Buy fishnet stockings with seams.
30. Get a two-hour massage.
31. Take piano lessons (unless, of course, you are Josie Natori).
32. Learn black-and-white photography.
33. Have a double-session scalp massage.
34. Buy a leopard-print minidress that's too tight and too short.
35. Get a dog.
36. Trade in your Aerostar for a Harley.
37. Buy a bunch of sex toys.
38. Write someone a passionate love letter.
39. Buy a bicycle.
40. Buy white cotton sheets, stay in bed all day, and watch Bette Davis movies.
41. Get your hair styled like Goldie Hawn.
42. Buy a hugely expensive pair of heels so high it is nearly impossible to walk in them.
43. Buy the most expensive bra and underpants in the world.

44. Take horseback riding lessons.

45. Ride a roller-coaster or six.

46. Learn to surf. Again.

47. Become a weight lifter. (Linda bench-presses 140 lbs.)

48. Start your own company—why should everyone else get the profits?

49. Go club hopping all night with your best friends and wear something that your kids disapprove of (see #34).

50. Do whatever the hell you want!

about the authors

LINDA STASI

Linda Stasi is a writer, newspaper columnist, and on-camera reporter. She's broken stories ranging from the first interview with a Gotti family member to the simultaneous interviews with Hillary Rodham Clinton and Gennifer Flowers, the first interview with New York State's incoming governor, George Pataki, and the last interview with the outgoing governor, Mario Cuomo.

Her series on female prisoners was responsible for changing the laws in New York State. She has been a columnist for

Newsday, The Daily News, and *The Village Voice.* She has been an on-camera contributing editor for TV's *Extra!*

She is the author of three books: *Simply Beautiful, Looking Good Is the Best Revenge,* and *A Field Guide to Impossible Men.*

Linda has been the beauty and health editor of *Cosmopolitan, New Woman,* and *Elle* and has written for *Ladies' Home Journal, Mademoiselle, McCall's,* and other magazines.

She produced a health and beauty program, *The Good Looks Line,* for four years and has been a regular contributor to many morning radio shows. Linda is now working as a screenwriter and columnist for *The Village Voice.*

Her TV appearances include *Oprah, Geraldo, Regis and Kathie Lee, Today,* and *Good Morning America.* She and her work were featured on *48 Hours* in a segment titled "Making News."

Linda is the single mother of one daughter, a twenty-two-year-old graduate of Wellesley College, and lives in New York City.

ROSEMARY ROGERS

Rosemary Rogers is an executive producer and founding partner of the New York music production company John Hill Music. The company, in business for seventeen years, creates original music for television and feature films. Besides music, she writes and produces comedy radio commercials for her company.

Rosemary is the coauthor, with Sean Kelly, of the best-selling humor/reference book *Saints Preserve Us!* She collaborated again with Kelly on its sequel, *Who in Hell . . .*, and the pair appeared on the *Today Show*, PBS, as well as several network radio talk shows to discuss heaven, hell, saints, demons, and comedy. They were part of the Toyoto Comedy Festival in 1995 and 1996.

Rosemary is the single mother of one daughter, a college sophomore at Vassar, and lives in New York City.